Ken Hanley's No Nonsense

Guide To Fly Fishing
In Northern California

A Quick, Clear Understanding of Fly Fishing
Northern California's Finest
Rivers, Lakes Reservoirs and Bays

Published by David Communications • 6171 Tollgate • Sisters, Oregon 97759

Acknowledgments

I'd like to show my gratitude to a few of my colleagues. Their talents and unselfish expertise are an integral part of this guide. **Andy Burk** and **Scott Saiki** are two of the most credible flyfishers plying the state's northern waters. Their daily ventures afield offer the latest fly fishing news. **Sandy Watts**, **Woody Woodland** and **Mike Mercer** were always available to discuss fly selection. **Glenn Kishi** did the fine work behind the camera.

This guidebook received advance review and improvements from fly fishers: **Ernie Kinzli** owner of Ernie's Casting Pond, **Kurt Lemons** owner of Upstream Flyfishing, **Bill Kiene, Ed Digardi**, **Alan Barnard** and **Andy Guibord** of Kiene's Fly Shop and, again, Andy Burk of The Fly Shop. Thanks' tons guys, your additions will help everyone enjoy fly fishing Northern California.

Finally, special thanks to Lynn Perrault, Denise Westmorland, Pete Chadwell and David Banks for taking my chicken scratches and turning them into a fine guidebook.

Ken Hanley's No Nonsense
Guide To Fly Fishing In Northern California

©1996 David Communications
ISBN #0-9637256-5-3

Published by David Communications
6171 Tollgate • Sisters, Oregon 97759 • U.S.A.

Printed by Griffin Printing
4141 N. Freeway Blvd. Sacramento, CA 95834

Author: Ken Hanley
Editor: David Banks
Cover Design: Lynn Perrault,
Denise Westmorland, David Banks
Illustrations: Pete Chadwell
Front Cover Photo: Glenn Kishi
Back Cover Photos: Glenn Kishi, Jane Mason

David Communications believes that in addition to local information and gear, fly fishers need fresh water and healthy fish. The publisher encourages preservation, improvement, conservation, enjoyment and understanding of our waters and their inhabitants. A good way to do this is to support organizations dedicated to these ideas.

David Communications is a member and sponsor of, and donor to Trout Unlimited, The Federation of Fly Fishers, Oregon Trout, California Trout, New Mexico Trout, American Rivers, Waterfowl U.S.A. and Ducks Unlimited. We encourage you to get involved, learn more and to join such organizations. Trout Unlimited 1(800) 834-2419 • Federation of Fly Fishers (406) 585-7592 • Oregon Trout (503) 222-9091 • California Trout (415) 392-8887 • New Mexico Trout (505) 344-6363 • American Rivers (202) 547-6900 • Ducks Unlimited: (901) 758-3825.

Disclaimer - While this guide will greatly help readers to fly fish, it is not a substitute for caution, good judgement and the services of a qualified guide or outfitter.

Manufactured in the United States of America

I dedicate this work to

Leon Berthiume, Dennis Johnson and Steve Yool.

They fueled my fire for sunrises and sunsets

atop the Sierra crest.

I also dedicate this guide to teachers past.

They gave me the gift to ask questions

and the tools to discover answers.

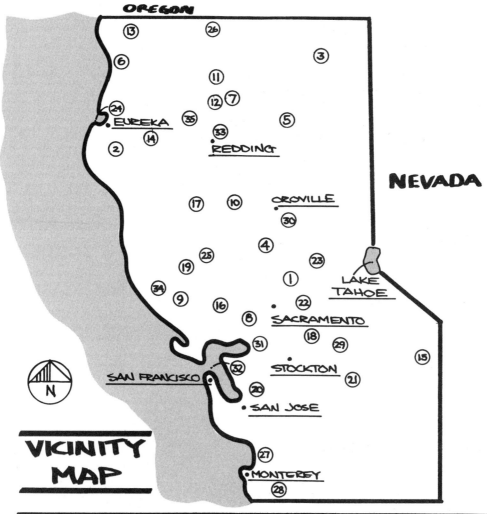

OREGON

NEVADA

⑬ ㉖
⑥ ③
⑪
⑫ ⑦
㉔ ㉟ ⑤
EUREKA
⑭
② ㉝
REDDING

⑰ ⑩ OROVILLE
㉚
④
⑲ ㉕ ㉓
① LAKE
TAHOE
㉞ ⑨ ⑯ ㉒
⑧ SACRAMENTO
㉛ ⑱ ㉙
⑮
SAN FRANCISCO ㉜ STOCKTON
㉑
⑳
SAN JOSE

VICINITY
MAP

N

㉗
MONTEREY
㉘

REFERENCED RIVERS, LAKES AND RESERVOIRS

1 AMERICAN RIVER
2 EEL RIVER
3 FALL RIVER
4 FEATHER RIVER
5 HAT CREEK
6 KLAMATH RIVER
7 McCLOUD RIVER
8 PUTAH CREEK
9 RUSSIAN RIVER
10 LOWER SACRAMENTO
11 UPPER SACRAMENTO (1)
12 UPPER SACRAMENTO (2)
13 SMITH RIVER
14 TRINITY RIVER
15 YOSEMITE NATIONAL PARK
16 LAKE BERRYESSA
17 BLACK BUTTE LAKE
18 LAKE CAMANCHE

19 CLEAR LAKE
20 DEL VALLE RESERVOIR
21 DON PEDRO LAKE
22 FOLSOM LAKE
23 FRENCH MEADOWS RES.
24 HUMBOLDT BAY
25 INDIAN VALLEY RESERVOIR
26 IRON GATE RESERVOIR
27 MONTEREY BAY
28 NACIMIENTO RESERVOIR
29 NEW HOGAN RESERVOIR
30 LAKE OROVILLE
31 SACRAMENTO/SAN JOAQUIN DELTAS
32 SAN FRANCISCO BAY
33 LAKE SHASTA
34 LAKE SONOMA
35 TRINITY LAKE

Contents

Section One
Selected Rivers & Streams

Section Two
Selected Lakes, Reservoirs & Saltwater

Appendix

Preface

I've been a guide, naturalist, and environmental educator since 1972. Fly fishing is one of the supreme tools of my trade and it has helped me to initiate, participate and communicate.

As an educator, I trade in information and answers. I value opportunities to facilitate an experience and I value the exchange of ideas. I conduct these exchanges in numerous venues: the classroom, the field, the show circuit and in my writing. This guide is a straightforward — no, my publisher corrects — this guide is a *No Nonsense* tool that combines my information and ideas in a way that will help you explore. At the least, this guide should inspire you to explore (and share) some of the marvelous natural wonders in Northern California.

Adventure recreation is another huge part of my life. I thrive on discovery and relish the great outdoor experience. Fly fishing, in many ways, is a window to this adventure. I look through the fly fishing pane and discover nature's beauty and harsh realities. This window helps open my mind as well as my spirit.

Northern California offers kelp beds, sandy beaches, mountain streams, valley rivers, alpine tarns, urban reservoirs, rainbow trout, striped bass, rockfish, salmon, steelhead, shad and more! What are we waiting for? Let's hit the road and fly fish the northern waters of the Golden State. Perhaps we'll have the pleasure of sharing a stream and sharing the dream.

No Nonsense

Northern California
FlyGuidelines

While compiling this guidebook I often made personal judgments about a water and location and its worthiness as a fly fishing destination. For balance, these judgments also represent the boiling down of information I've gained from others. I then stirred in my own adventures and history (with these waters) to write a guide that reflects what I *know*.

Let me be the first to say that my experiences afield will likely be different from yours. I have no doubt that many of you are more aggressive, technically talented and down right luckier than I have been. Your experiences have influenced your judgments of waters in ways completely different from my experiences. Therefore, this guide (or any other for that matter) is a reflection of *ongoing* Northern California fly fishing experiences.

Everyone who cares to have one, has a perspective on the subject of fly fishing around here. They're all valid and worth tossing into the mix of information. Opinions aside, this guide will get you into some of the best fly fishing waters in Northern California that I can recommend. Cheers to past encounters and future trips.

Information

Because Northern California has so much to offer the fly fisher, it's important to do a little homework before hitting the road. First, read this guide. Then dial up one of the contact numbers in the appendix section. A simple phone call might give you some scouting info that's your ticket to success. Call area fly shops, guides, clubs and park services. These resources deal with specific waters almost daily. Their information is generally very accurate and should help in your decision to venture off with fly rod in hand.

Ratings

How do you rate your last fly fishing outing? You consider the weather, the company, water, access, gamefish, a great cast and presentation, almost everything. When retelling your experience, aside from where you had lunch, the 3 most helpful comments for others include access, gamefish and water quality.

The 1 to 10 rating scale in this guide employs these considerations. Anything rated an "8" or above represents the highest quality water and is a "must" for any flyfisher in the Golden State. A "1" rating would be atrocious. I haven't even considered these waters for this guidebook.

Ratings - continued

All waters in this guide rate a "5" or better. Keep in mind that the scale is a stepping stone of sorts. Develop your own ratings the day you're on the water!

The fish at the bottom of each page indicate the water's rating. You get an impression of the water at a glance.

Regulations

The regulations sited in this guide are based on the *Department of Fish and Game's California Sport Fishing Regulations*, dated March 1994 through February 1996. With the complex conservation practices in our state, you can be sure that the regulations will change from time to time. Please refer to the State's latest edition to be safe. And don't forget your fishing license.

Hatches & Baitfish

This guide doesn't pretend to be a Western entomology or baitfish cycle authority. Those subjects can fill volumes of encyclopedias. The hatches and baitfish mentioned in this guide are a basic reference that will help you to assemble your tackle. When the hatch cycle is consistent and reliable, it's mentioned. The main food items that gamefish key on are here. If you can't find exactly what you need, contact one of the resources listed in the appendix for specifics.

Fly Fishing
In Northern California
Thoughts on New Ideas, Crowds, Regulations and Contributions

The Golden State is a huge fly fishing puzzle composed of very diverse fishing areas and experiences. All the pieces fit together because of the commonalty of the fly rod. At times, however, many have to abandon tradition and experiment with different tackle and techniques. This is after all, *California* where this type of boldness is common. I believe you'll find that these challenges and rewards will make your time afield most memorable.

Northern California has its share of "Blue Ribbon" waters. As you might expect, these locations draw a great deal of attention and pressure. I often hear statements that begin with "California's streams are so crowded...blah, blah, blah.".

My reply, "You've got to be kidding!"

There's hundreds of fishable streams and rivers and over half a million acres of stillwater in the northern part of the state. The coastline stretches nearly a thousand miles and the delta systems have over a thousand miles of navigable waterways! If the river's too crowded, find another piece of the fly fishing puzzle to enjoy. There's absolutely no reason to feel crowded unless you choose to be in that situation. I don't mean to be critical, but the point is, **move around**. We have a huge area that few make any effort to discover. ...Whew. I feel better now.

Moving around helps with angling conservation too. Rotating your destinations reduces or minimizes your impact on any single resource. It's a "win / win" deal. You'll experience the joys of new waters while giving your favorite locations a chance to recover. Whenever someone comments about crowds, smile and say "That's just not true where I've cast my lines."

Back to the puzzle that is fly fishing in Northern California. The California Department of Fish and Game, conservation groups and businesses help to make it all possible. The task is demanding, the stakes are high and the questions difficult. For example, should we continue to have a Striped Bass Rearing Program with the potential loss of salmon fry? Do we designate the upper Sacramento River a trophy catch-and-release stream or operate it as a put-n-take fishery? Should we reduce the season on our coastal steelhead streams?

These complex fishery problems and solutions are an ongoing experiment. The D.F.G. has its hands full indeed. Your help is necessary to assure the future for high quality angling experiences. Please get involved. Without your assistance we don't have a chance. Here are a few ways you can make a positive contribution to fly fishing in Northern California.

- Abide by the laws.
- Respect property rights.
- Catch and release wild fish.
- Don't crowd a fellow angler.
- Carry out your, and someone else's, litter.
- Take a friend or the family fly fishing.
- If you harvest fish, limit your catch don't catch your limit.

A No Nonsense Display of
Proven Winners for
Northern California Waters

These flies and streamers are available at flyshops throughout the state and by mail order.

Steelhead

SILVER HILTON

BOSS

BRINDLE BUG

GLO BUG

Trout (Lakes)

ZONKER

CLOUSER MINNOW

MARABOU DRAGON

DAMSEL NYMPH

WOOLY BUGGER

ADULT MIDGE

MIDGE PUPA

Trout (Streams)

LITTLE YELLOW STONEFLY

ADAMS

BLACK FUR ANT

GOLD-RIBBED HARE'S EAR

BLUE WINGED OLIVE

PHEASANT TAIL

BIRD'S NEST

ELK HAIR CADDIS

Bass

THREADFIN SHAD

WHITLOCK DEER HAIR POPPER

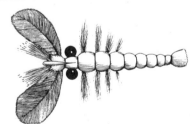

WHITLOCK'S CRAYFISH

V-WORM

BLANTON WHISTLER

Saltwater

POPOVIC'S SURF CANDY

BLANTON'S SAR-MUL-MAC

CLOUSER MINNOW DEEP WATER

LEFTY'S DECEIVER

Illustrations by Pete Chadwell. For fine art and fish renderings write to: Dynamic Arts • 1832 N.E. Providence Dr. • Bend, OR 97701 ❖ **xi** ❖

A No Nonsense Display of
Common Game Fish In Northern California

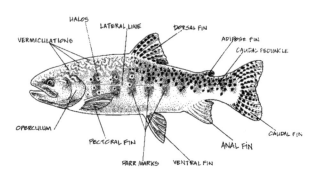

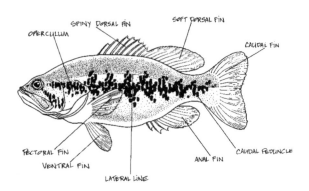

Typical salmon, trout or char. Most hatchery fish have a clipped adipose fin.

Typical bass, perch, crappie or rock fish.

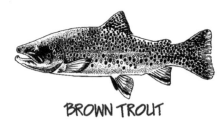

BROWN TROUT

Brown colored back with big black spots. A square tail and black and red spots on sides with light blue rings. Hard to catch, easily spooked.

BROOK TROUT

'Brookies' are in the char family (Dolly Varden, Bull Trout, Lake Trout etc.). Back colors are black, blue-gray or green with mottled light colored markings. Sides have red spots with blue rings. Square tail. Lower fins are red and striped with black and white. Found in colder waters.

RAINBOW TROUT

The most abundant wild and hatchery fish. An olive-bluish back with small black spots. Sides have light red or pink band. Lake 'bows' are often all silver.

CHINOOK SALMON

Male Chinook or King (shown), has dark brown back that reflects purple in the sun with large black angular spots. Spotted upper and lower powerful square tail. Jaws curl (kype) during spawning. Mouth and gums are dark.

STEELHEAD TROUT

These trout leave rivers for the ocean and return to spawn several times. Similar to rainbows but with fewer spots, bigger and stronger. The tongue tip has teeth, but not the tongue back. Great fighting fish.

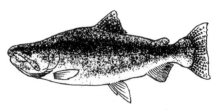

COHO SALMON

Male Coho or Silver (shown), has blue-green back with small round spots covering only the back and upper caudal fin. Jaws curl (kype) during spawning. Mouth lining dark except white areas on gums at teeth.

A No Nonsense Display of

Common Game Fish In Northern California

AMERICAN SHAD

Bluish silver back and silver-white sides. Faint spots on sides above lateral line. Small head in relation to overall body size. Split tail. Largest of the Herrings, the anadromous "poor-man's Tarpon" is a real fighter.

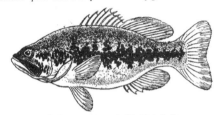

LARGEMOUTH BASS

Dark green back and sides with dark band of diamond-like shapes along sides. Spiny dorsal fin (9-10 rays) separated from soft dorsal fin by deep notch. Closed upper jaw extends to rear or beyond rear of eyes.

SMALLMOUTH BASS

Dark brown back with vertical bronze stripes on the sides. Spiny dorsal fin (9-10 spines) hasn't a deep notch separating the soft dorsal fin. Closed upper jaw doesn't extend past the eyes.

STRIPED BASS

Greenish back, 7-8 horizontal stripes on silver background on sides. Spiny dorsal fin attached to soft dorsal. Longer than other bass, "stripers" can grow to over 50 lbs.

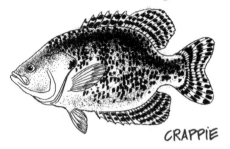

CRAPPIE

Silver and greenish with dark green or black splotches on the sides. Compressed body with upturned snout. Spines on dorsal, anal fins.

SURF PERCH

Several varieties range from light silver to olive brown. Spiny dorsal fins. Elliptical body, height almost equal to length. Mouth like Crappie. Found in surf zone and areas with sandy bottom or rock lined shore.

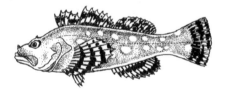

CABEZON

Wide body, head and shoulders, tapering to tail. Camouflage pattern of dark reddish-brown colors. Large mouth and pectoral fins. Prefers rocks near bottom, not open water.

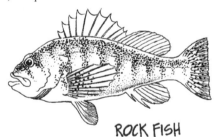

ROCK FISH

Olive, blue to black, similar to a freshwater bass. Powerful broom-like tail, large sharp fins. Likes rocky shallows, kelp beds and breakwaters.

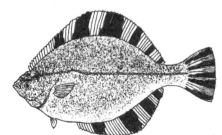

Flat fish have a large flat body and small eyes on top of the head, and sharp teeth. Halibut have gray back, silver-white belly. Prefer the surf zone. Smaller Flounder has darker skin with mottled brown pattern on back. Found in estuaries, sloughs and surf.

STARRY FLOUNDER

Illustrations by Pete Chadwell. For fine art and fish renderings write to: Pete Chadwell •1832 N.E. Providence Dr. • Bend, OR 97701.

Section One
Selected Rivers
&
Streams

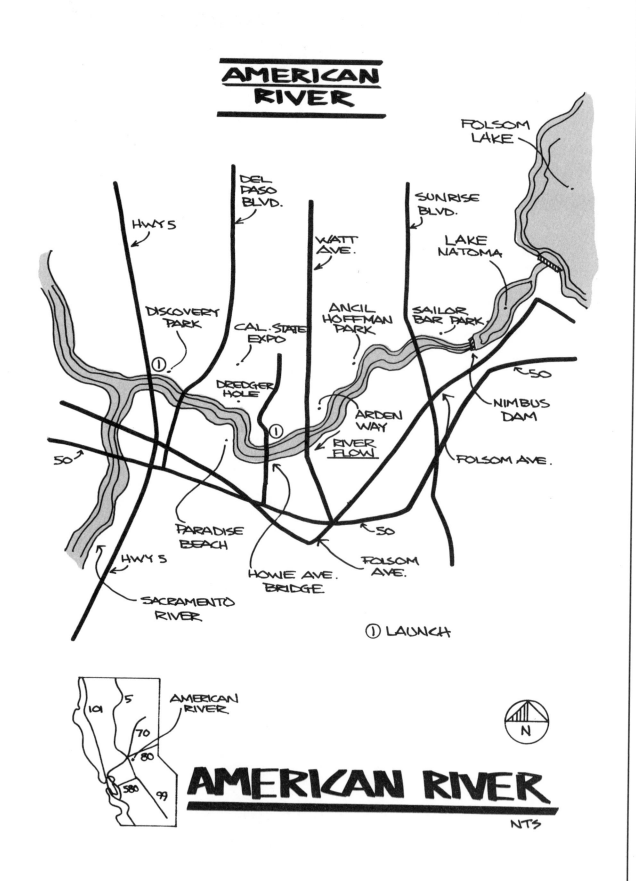

AMERICAN RIVER

FOLSOM LAKE

DEL PASO BLVD.

SUNRISE BLVD.

HWY 5

WATT AVE.

LAKE NATOMA

DISCOVERY PARK

CAL. STATE EXPO

ANCIL HOFFMAN PARK

SAILOR BAR PARK

① LAUNCH

DREDGER HOLE

50

NIMBUS DAM

50

ARDEN WAY

RIVER FLOW

FOLSOM AVE.

PARADISE BEACH

50

HWY 5

HOWE AVE. BRIDGE

FOLSOM AVE.

SACRAMENTO RIVER

① LAUNCH

AMERICAN RIVER

101 5

AMERICAN RIVER

70

80

580 99

AMERICAN RIVER

NTS

N

The American River
Lower Section

A wonderful 22 mile tailwater fishery flows right through the heart of California's state capitol and into the Sacramento River. And believe it or not, the lower American gets less overall pressure than a place like Fall River during peak season! Keep in mind, however, there are millions of potential anglers near this stretch of river. It's urban fly fishing on the lower American, but worth the adventure.

The American doesn't have trout, but it does have a variety of gamefish that are hearty and challenging. Combining resident and anadromous species, the river offers a chance to try for fish ranging from 1 to 30 or more pounds.

Boaters tend to get the most from this river. Anyone with a canoe, pram, or small skiff will enjoy the many easy-to-get-to access points. Boat traffic and snags present hazards float tube users should heed. Many "Tubers" find a way to anchor themselves when they find high quality fly fishing locations. Bank anglers gain access around Discovery and Goethe Park, Cal Expo, Arden Way, Howe and Watt Avenue bridges and at Sunrise Avenue. It's good to call ahead to check the levels of the dam regulated river flows. The Sacramento-area fly shops listed in the back of this guide will help.

The easy way to get to this section of river is to take Highway 50 to the suburbs of Fair Oaks and Rancho Cordova. From here there are many surface streets that take one to the river.

Types of Fish
Smallmouth, redeye and striped bass, shad, steelhead and salmon (Chinook), plus crappie, bluegill and catfish..

When to Fish
Smallmouth & redeye bass: All year, prime time is spring and fall.
Striped bass: All year, prime time, July- Oct.
Shad: Mid-spring - June.
Steelhead: September - March.
Salmon: August - October.

Known Baitfish
Threadfin shad, gamefish fry and crawdads.

Equipment to Use
Rods: 6 - 8 weight, 8 1/2 - 10'.
Reels: Mechanical or palm drag. 75 yards backing for striped bass.
Lines: For deepwater nymphs and streamers, Hi-speed, Hi-D sink tip, #4 density uniform sinking line, shooting head system (sinking). Floating shooting head, or full floating line for poppers and shallow streamer work.
Leaders: primarily 1x to 5x, 6 - 9', lengths vary with river condition.
Wading: Chest-high waders and boots for bank angling.

Flies to Use
Streamers: Bullet Head #6, Woolly Bugger #2-10, assorted colors, Zonker #2-6.
Shad: Assorted colors Shad flies #6, Poxybou Crayfish #4-8, White or Gray Clouser Minnow #4-6.
Topwater: Chartreuse Gaines Popper #8, Madame X #6, Whitlock Hopper #8.

Boat Access
Sailor Bar Park, Sunrise, El Manto, Rosmore, Ancile Hoffman Park, Gristmill, Watt Ave., Howe Ave., Discovery Park (mouth).

Accommodations & Services
Lodging and supplies in Sacramento. Boating access at Discovery Park, Howe Avenue and Nimbus Basin.

Seasons & Limits
Restrictions on tackle and harvest vary. Consult the California Department of Fish and Game regulations booklet.

Rating
Overall, a 7.5.

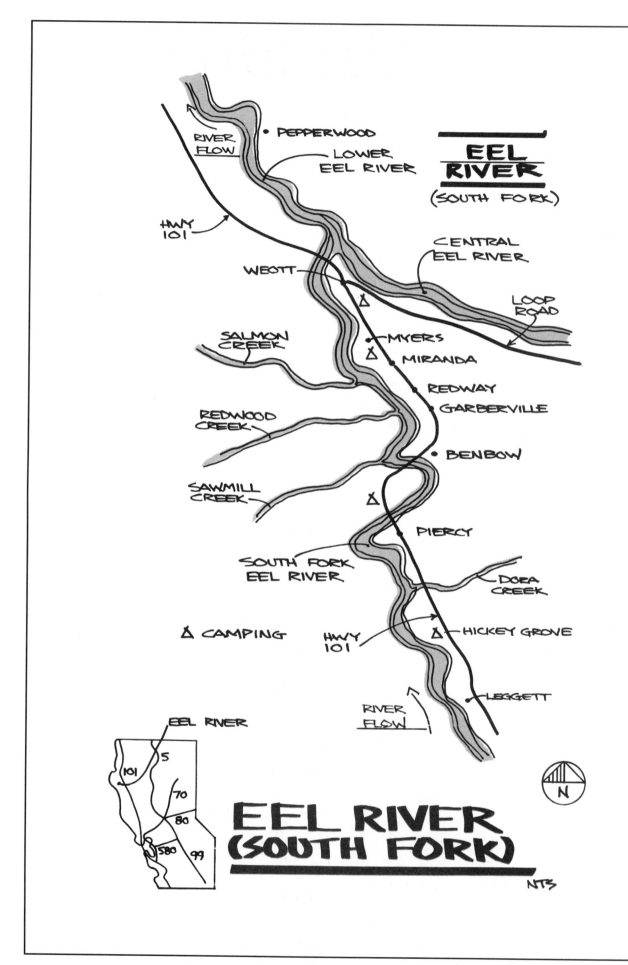

EEL RIVER
(SOUTH FORK)

The Eel River

The Eel is a terrific river system for fly fishers who are afoot or afloat. It's also one of the longest (100 miles) and prettiest stream corridors on the Northern California coastline. The beautiful fir, redwood and other trees that line the river and access along Highway 101 are remarkable. One can fly fish the river just about anywhere, from the tidewater environs to the upper waters at the town of Leggett.

As with any coastal fishery, the river is susceptible to flooding during heavy rains. The Eel usually needs anywhere from a few days to a week to clear. When the river is in prime condition your odds of tangling with a metallic steelhead or hefty Pacific salmon are first-rate. Check the slow moving sections of river and deep holes for salmon. Check behind big rocks and in tailouts for steelhead. Fishing from a drift boat for steelhead usually provides the most success. The angler willing to "travel the system" is most likely to find the active fish. To check stream closures try the D.F.&G. recorded message, (707) 442-4502.

During the warmer months shad show up in the lower river. The runs have become sporadic and weak in recent years. Call a fly shop to time the shad fishery. Also, the Eel can get very low in the summer, all but eliminating fishing.

To get to this fishery just use Highway 101. Access from the north will be along approximately 90 miles of our dramatic coastline, past the towns of Crescent City, Arcata and Eureka. Travelers from the south pass through San Francisco, Santa Rosa, Ukiah, Willits and Leggett. The drive is roughly 200 miles from the San Francisco Bay Area.

Types of Fish
King salmon (Chinook), silver salmon (Coho), steelhead, shad.

When to Fish
Kings: October - early January, prime time is late Nov - Dec.
Silvers: October - December, prime time is Oct - Nov. Not a large run.
Steelhead: November - March, prime time is Dec - Feb.
Shad: Late spring - Summer, in the lower river.

Known Hatches
Concentrate on fly selection. In tidewater environs use baitfish and shrimp patterns. Inland sections use traditional "spawn" patterns and attractor style streamers and nymphs.

Equipment to Use
Rods: 7 - 9 weight, 8 -10'.
Reels: Mechanical drag.
Lines: Sinking shooting head system or sink-tip lines. 150 - 300 grain wt.
Leaders: 1x - 3x, 6- 10'.
Wading: Chest-high neoprene waders, felt soled boots. Dress for "cold & wet" in winter.

Flies to Use
Tidewater area
Streamers: Polar Shrimp #6, Krystal Bullet #4-6, Fall Favorite #2, silver/blue, silver, silver/red baitfish patterns #2.

Main Stream
Streamers: Boss #4-10, Brindle Bug #6-10, Glo Bug #6, Silver Hilton #6-10, Green-butt Skunk #4-10.

Accommodations & Services
Lodging, food and supplies in Fortuna, Rio Dell, Garberville and Leggett. Public and private campgrounds in Rio Dell, Weott, Myers Flat, Benbow and the Leggett area.

Nearby Fly Fishing
Try the Van Duzen river.

Seasons & Limits
This river is subject to low flow closure. Restrictions include tackle, harvest, and access and can change from season to season. Consult California fishing regulations.

Rating
If the river stays in shape in winter, this can be a real winner. Overall, a 6.5.

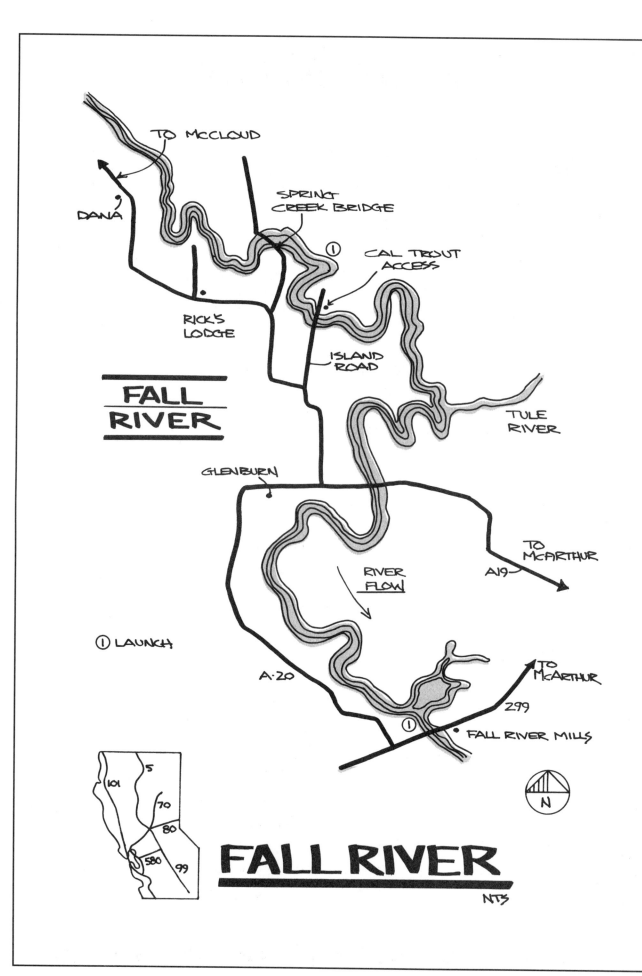

TO McCLOUD

DANA

SPRING CREEK BRIDGE

CAL TROUT ACCESS

RICK'S LODGE

ISLAND ROAD

TULE RIVER

FALL RIVER

GLENBURN

TO McARTHUR

A19

RIVER FLOW

① LAUNCH

A·20

TO McARTHUR

299

FALL RIVER MILLS

5

101

70

80

580

99

N

FALL RIVER

NTS

Fall River

This is Northern California trout water at it's finest. If you enjoy cool, clear, deep running classic spring-fed mountain rivers with thick and lush mats of vegetation, Fall River just might be your ticket to trout heaven. You'll need a boat or float tube to fly fish the best areas, however, as the majority of the bank access is through private property. Prams and John boats with electric motors are best for working this wide (100-250 yards) and spacious waterway. A two anchor system is a good way to help position ones boat. For the first-timer, a guide is the best way to learn this river.

Fall River was originally used to transport logs and was virtually a private watercourse. Anglers had limited access until the early 1970's. Today, flyfishers enjoy a bonus from the logging days. Many "sinker" logs provide sunken cover and prime habitat for trout. These hefty, strong-fighting, wild trout run 16-20". The average trout weighs 2-3 lbs. Every year enough 6-11 lb. monsters are hooked to keep anglers on their toes!

Most flyfishers use a down-and-across presentation of short casts with line mends that extend the drift. This technique has earned the moniker "Fall River Twitch". Drag-free drifts and long leaders are critical for both nymph and dry fly presentations. Remember, this river is smooth, has little pocket water and few rifles.

Highway 5 is the ticket to this wonderful fishery. Traveling from the north, as you pass the town of Mt. Shasta, keep an eye open for the McCloud Exit, Highway 89. Follow 89 until it intersects 299. There travel east on 299 to Fall River Mills. A-20 then takes one right to Glenburn and all the action. From the south take Highway 5 into the city of Redding. Exit onto 299 East and drive directly to Fall River Mills. The river is about a 6 hour drive from the Bay Area.

Types of Fish
Brown and rainbow trout.

Known Hatches
Spring & Fall: Baetis (Pale Morning Dun, Blue Winged Olive).
June: Hexagenia Mayfly, PMD.
July - August: Green Drake, caddis, PMD.
All year: Scuds, leeches.

Equipment to Use
Rods: 4 - 6 weight, 7 - 9 1/2'.
Reels: Mechanical or palm drag.
Lines: Floating. For deep water, sink tip rated #2 or 130 grains.
Leaders: 5x to 8x, 10 - 15' for surface.
4x to 5x, 7 - 9' for subsurface.
Wading: Take a boat for more fly fishing opportunities.

Flies to Use
Nymphs: Olive Bird's Nest #12-14, Hunched Back Infrequens (HBI) #16-20, PT #16-20, Green Sparkle Pupa #16-18, Damselfly Nymph #10-12, Scuds #10-16, Poxyback Green Drake #12, Zug Bug #14-18, Hexagenia #6.

Dries: Tan or Olive Paradun #16-20, Trico #18-20, Brown Elk Hair Caddis #14-16, Henryville Special #16, Hexagenia May #6, Olive or Brown Mayfly Emerger #16-20.

Streamers: Olive or Brown Woolly Bugger #8-#10.

When to Fish
Fish for rainbows and browns all season. Late-summer and fall are the best times of year for browns.

Seasons & Limits
Barbless artificials only, 2 fish under 14". Seasons and regulations change, always check at a local fly shop.

Accommodations & Services
Lodging and supplies in Burney, Glenburn and Fall River Mills.

Rating
A great river on which to build "visual" skills such as interpreting feeding behavior, holding lies, current seams, etc. Easily a 9.

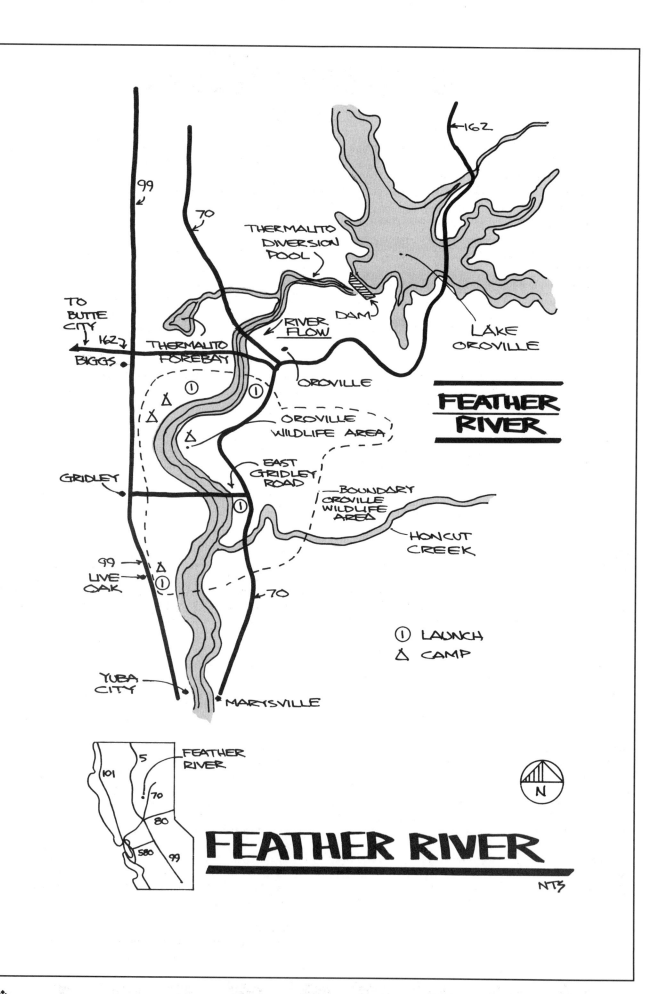

FEATHER RIVER

162

THERMALITO
DIVERSION
POOL

LAKE
OROVILLE

TO
BUTTE
CITY
162

BIGGS

THERMALITO
FOREBAY

RIVER
FLOW

DAM

OROVILLE

OROVILLE
WILDLIFE AREA

GRIDLEY

EAST
GRIDLEY
ROAD

BOUNDARY
OROVILLE
WILDLIFE
AREA

HONCUT
CREEK

99
LIVE
OAK

70

① LAUNCH
△ CAMP

YUBA
CITY

MARYSVILLE

99

70

FEATHER
RIVER

101

5

70

80

580

99

N

FEATHER RIVER

NTS

Feather River

Lower Section

The Lower Feather spills out of Lake Oroville and runs 50 miles south through the Central Valley. This beautiful river way contains about a dozen different gamefish including a number of anadromous species. Part of the fun here is picking the type of fish one wishes to pursue. In nearly every month of the year fly fishing on the Feather can put a smile on your face. Before the Oroville dam was built the Lower Feather was one of the states' top salmon rivers.

As a general rule, the upper stretches run shallow and fast (over bedrock), while the lower river is wide, deep, and slow. Boaters have an advantage from Yuba City to Verona and the confluence with the Sacramento River. Bank angling access is best around Shanghai Bend and from Gridley Bridge to Thermolito Afterbay. The Oroville Wildlife Area offers more foot access, and farther downstream wading is possible in the Live Oak area. There are wadeable areas below the town of Yuba City as well. The best access is during low water periods.

The lower Feather holds a great population of year-round smallmouth bass. Look for them anywhere there is bass-type cover: logs, brush, stumps, undercut banks etc. April - May is the best time for these 1 to 2 pounders.

Most anglers take Highway 5 from Sacramento (heading toward Marysville and Yuba City) to get to the Feather. To work the eastern shore, follow highway 70 into Marysville and towards Oroville. To access the western shore, take the 99 split into Yuba City, through Live Oak, Gridley and Biggs. Local surface roads provide numerous access points to the water. Sacramento to Yuba City/Marysville is about 45 miles. The drive into Oroville from the capitol is close to 70 miles.

Types of Fish
Shad, smallmouth bass, striped bass, salmon, steelhead and rainbow trout.

Known Baitfish
Salmon roe, gamefish fry, sculpins and crawdads.

Shad: April - August, prime time is June-July.
Smallmouth bass: all year, prime time is fall and spring.
Striped bass: March - June, prime time is April-May.
Salmon: October and January.
Steelhead: Sept. - Feb., prime time is October.

Equipment to Use
Rods: 6 - 8 weight, 8 - 9 1/2'.
Reels: Mechanical drag with 50 yards of backing for large fish.
Lines: Hi-speed, Hi-D sink-tip for fast flows or deeper presentations. For streamers, #4 density uniform sinking line, 130 or 200 grain shooting head. Floating line for low water or poppers.
Leaders: 3x to 5x, 6 - 10'.
Wading: Chest-high neoprene waders, studded boots, wading staff. Hip boots OK for bank angling. A boat provides more fly fishing opportunities.

Flies to Use
Streamers: Olive or White Thunder Creek Marabou #2-6, Woolly Bugger #2-10, Muddler Minnow #2-8, Zonker #2-6, Poxybou Crayfish #4-8, Shad Fly #6, Red & White Blanton's Flashtail Whistler #3/0.
Other: Glo Bug #6-8.
Topwater: Olive, Yellow, Chartreuse Gaines Popper #8.

When to Fish
In general, for hefty monsters like King salmon and stripers, or sleek steelhead and shad, fish spring - fall. Fish for smallmouth bass, trout and panfish all year long.

Seasons & Limits
Restrictions on access, tackle, harvest and species vary throughout the year and river system. Always consult California fishing regulations or a fly shop.

Accommodations & Services
Boat access at various spots along the river. Launch ramp and supplies available at Verona Marina. Camping at Lake Oroville State Recreation Area. Lodging and supplies available in Oroville, Marysville and Yuba City.

Rating
Crowds can build in the more popular runs during a hot bite period, but overall, an 8.5.

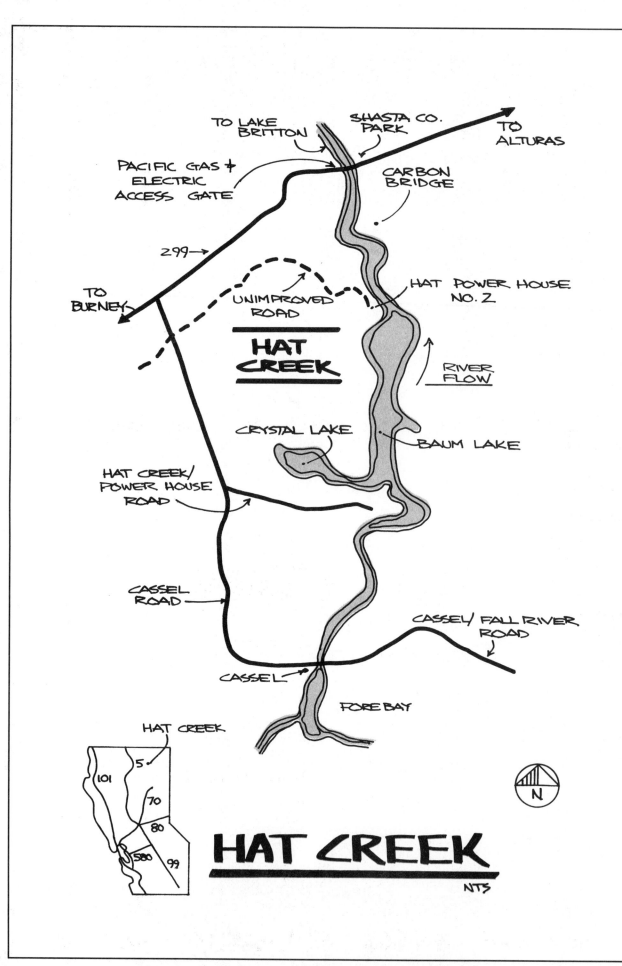

TO LAKE BRITTON

SHASTA CO. PARK

TO ALTURAS

PACIFIC GAS & ELECTRIC ACCESS GATE

CARBON BRIDGE

299 →

HAT POWER HOUSE NO. 2

TO BURNEY

UNIMPROVED ROAD

HAT CREEK

RIVER FLOW

CRYSTAL LAKE

BAUM LAKE

HAT CREEK/ POWER HOUSE ROAD

CASSEL ROAD

CASSEL/ FALL RIVER ROAD

CASSEL

FORE BAY

HAT CREEK

5

101

70

80

580

99

N

HAT CREEK

NTS

Hat Creek

With headwaters in Lassen Volcanic National Park, Upper Hat Creek is a rumbling, mountain stream. Fish here with all forms of flies, lures and bait. Anglers can camp steamside and haul in all sorts of hatchery trout.

In the valley, highly regarded Lower Hat Creek is a Blue Ribbon meadow-meander. It's classified a Wild Trout stream. This 3.5 mile of river has all the ingredients many fly rodders dream about. Gin clear water. Tricky currents. Wild fish. Complex food chain. Add this up and you've quite a fly fishing test on a world-class trout stream.

In 1968 all non-game fish were purged of the lower river, which was then replanted with native and wild trout. Regulation changes, a halt to fish stocking and natural propagation has resulted in an outstanding population of wild trout. Hat Creek and Fall River are perhaps California's (if not the West's) best, classic fly fishing streams.

The Lower Hat features extraordinarily long, glassy and deep pools and a series of shallow riffles. The streambed has lots of cover concealing wary trout that average 10-16". The banks are verdant, with hardwoods and shrubs and a mixture of grasses. Hatches are many and often nearly simultaneous. Don't limit yourself to dry fly action as sight nymphing can be dynamite on this river!

Hat Creek "central" is the town of Burney, 51 miles east of Redding (I-5) on Highway 299. At Burney take 299 northeast about 8 miles to the stream.

Types of Fish
Rainbow and brown trout.

Known Hatches
April-May: Salmon Fly and Golden Stones, PMD.
May - June: Green Drakes, Pale Morning, Pale Evening Dun, Caddis.
July - August: Baetis (BWO), Trico, Little Yellow Stone, Caddis.
September - October: Large October caddis.
All year: Small caddis.

Equipment to Use
Rods: 3 - 5 weight, 7 1/2 - 9'.
Reels: Mechanical or palm drag.
Lines: Floating. For deep water and caddis pupa, Hi-speed, Hi-D sink-tip
Leaders: 4x to 7x, 10 - 12' or longer.
Wading: Chest-high neoprene waders, felt-soled boots.

Flies to Use
Nymphs: Bird's Nest #14, Hare's Ear Beadhead #10-14, Hunched Back Infrequens "HBI" #16-18, PT #16-18, Green Rockworm #12, Poxyback Golden Stone & PMD #6-8, Black Rubberlegs #6, October Caddis Emerger #6, Green Sparkle Pupa #14.

Streamers: Olive Matuka Sculpin #2-6, Muddler Minnow #2-8.

Dries: Mahogany Dun #18, Harrop Haystack Callibaetis #14-16, Loopwing Paradun Olive #20, Tricos #20, Burk's CDC Stone #14, Brown Elk Hair Caddis #14, Orange or Gold Stimulator #8, Dave's Hopper #8-10, Yellow Humpy #4, Black Ant #12-14, Brown or Olive Mayfly Emerger #16-20, Green Drake Paradrake #8-10, various mayfly cripples and spinners.

When to Fish
May and October is prime time. Mornings and evenings and hatch periods are usually the best time of day to fly fish, especially in the summer.

Seasons & Limits
Usually open the last Saturday in April through November 15th. Upper Hat, limit five fish. Lower Hat, from Lake Britton to Power House #2, barbless flies and lures only, 2 fish, 18" minimum. Special restrictions on harvest and tackle can change so always check with a fly shop or the California fishing regulations booklet.

Accommodations & Services
Lodging, fly shops and supplies in Burney, Cassel and Fall River Mills. Camping is best at McArthur-Burney Falls Memorial State Park or the PG&E Camp in Cassel. A fine option is the Clearwater House Bed & Breakfast in Cassel.

Rating
On the upper section a 7, on the lower reaches an 8.5.

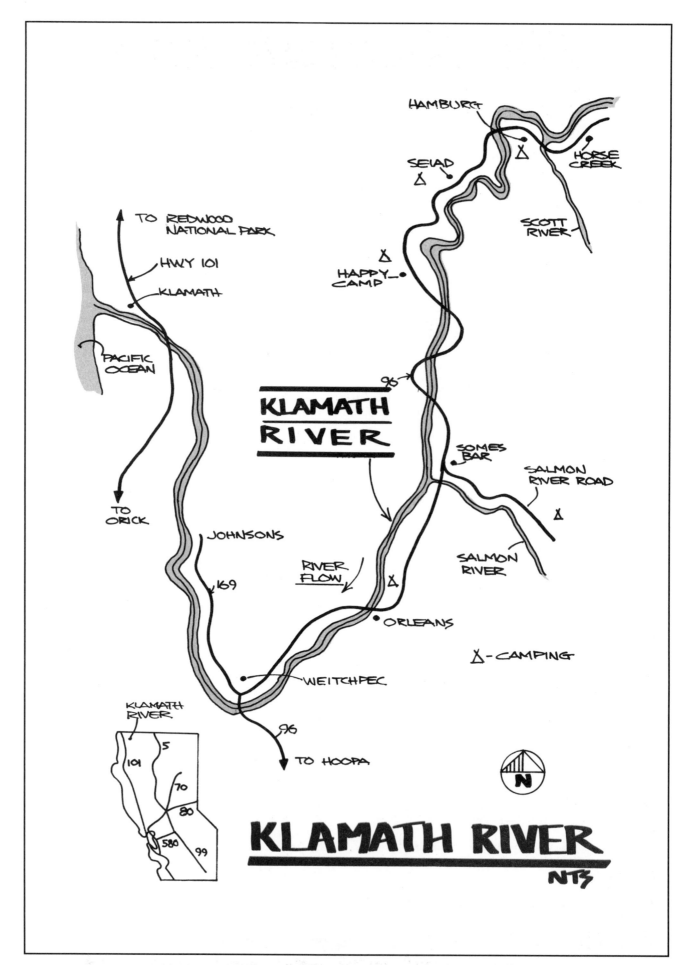

KLAMATH RIVER

NTS

The Klamath River

The Klamath is one of the great and historic Blue Ribbon rivers in the U.S. Thick timber, rough canyons, wildlife and a fishing friendly local economy create a beautiful and comprehensive setting for the fly fisher.

This is 200 miles of big river: big pools, big currents, big structure, big schools and thankfully, big fish. There can also be big crowds, but there's big space. Some of the best fly fishing is on the lower river: from the town of Weitchpec to the ocean. This region is vast (100-200' across) so you'll need a boat to access the prime waters.

Upriver, from Johnson's Bar to Hamburg, there's plenty of bank angling. Drive Highway 96 and look for likely spots. Fall and spring are peak periods for steelhead. Use floating-line, sink-tip, "greased-line" streamer presentations. The middle river is a popular 1 to 3 day float trip section. The 40 miles of upper river (Iron Gate Dam to Hamburg) has lengthy riffles and extensive pools. There's plenty of shore access. Steelhead run here from about September to March.

For salmon, use deep nymph and attractor techniques and heavy, sinking lines. Come May and June, the Shad runs offer terrific action for fly rodders. Look for schools moving in the tidewater and lower river systems. In late summer large concentrations of fish usually show up around the Ishi Pishi Falls area.

The Klamath starts below the dam at Iron Gate Reservoir, just east of Highway 5 and north of the city of Yreka. Highway 96 runs along most of the river. The mouth of the Klamath is located off of Highway 101, 20 miles south of Crescent City.

Types of Fish
King salmon (Chinook), steelhead, shad and trout.

Known Baitfish & Hatches
Various baitfish, isopods and shrimp in the tidewaters. Upstream imitate minnows and various nymphs for salmon and steelhead.

Equipment to Use
Steelhead
Rods: 5 - 9 weight, 8 1/2 - 91/2'.
Reels: Mechanical drag with lots of backing.
Lines: Floating, shooting heads or sink-tip.
Leaders: 0x - 3x, 7 -9'.
Wading: Chest-high neoprene waders, felt soled boots and a wading staff.
Salmon
Rods: 6 - 8 weight, 8 1/2 - 10'.
Reels: Mechanical drag with lots of backing.
Lines: Shooting heads or sink-tip.
Leaders: 0x or 1x, 7 -9'.
Wading: Same as above.
Trout
Rods: 4 - 7 weight, 8 1/2 - 91/2'.
Reels: Mechanical or palm drag.
Lines: Floating, or sink-tip to match rod weight.
Leaders: 4x or 5x, 7 -9'.
Wading: Same as for steelhead.

Flies to Use
Streamers: Gandalf's Touch #4-6, Bucktail Coachman #6, Burlap, Brindle Bug, Silver Hilton, Black Bear/Green-Butt #6-10, Purple Peril #6, Boss #4-10, Double Egg Sperm #4-8, Woolhead Sculpin #4, bead-eye style Shad patterns #6-12.

Nymphs: Dark Scud #12-14, Prince Black Bomber #10-12, Red Fox Squirrel #10-14, Gold Bead Bird's Nest #12, Golden Stone #6-10, Rubberlegs #4-6, Woolly Bugger #6, G-R Hare's Ear #8-12.

Drys: Madam X #6-8, Steelhead Caddis #8, Burk's Orange Krystal Waker #8.

When to Fish
Salmon: Summer and Fall.
Steelhead: Fall & Spring, prime time is Sept. - mid-Nov.
Shad: May - September, prime time is June-July.
Trout: Primarily in the upper river. Refer to state regs.

Seasons & Limits
The Klamath is subject to low flow and closure, restrictions on tackle, harvest and access. Consult current California DF&G fishing regulations or inquire at a local fly shop.

Accommodations & Services
Lodging and supplies are available in Happy Camp, Orleans and Klamath Glen. Camping is best near Hamburg, Seiad Valley, Happy Camp, Dillon Creek, Bluff Creek and the Orleans area.

Rating
In fall it can get a bit crowded for the bank angler, but overall the Klamath is an 8.

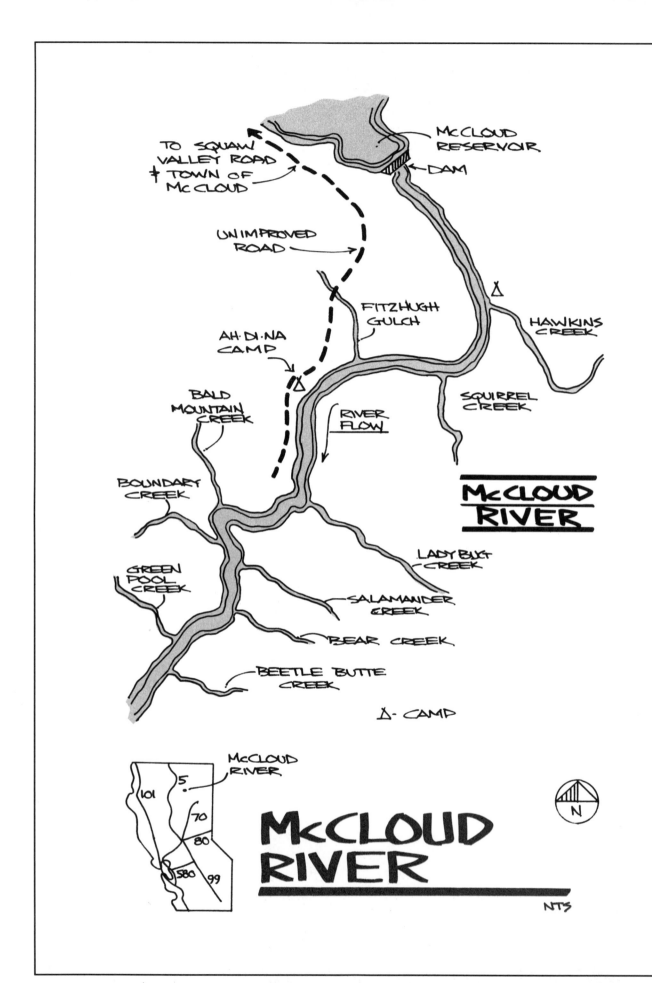

McCLOUD RESERVOIR

DAM

TO SQUAW VALLEY ROAD & TOWN OF McCLOUD

UNIMPROVED ROAD

FITZHUGH GULCH

HAWKINS CREEK

AH·DI·NA CAMP

SQUIRREL CREEK

BALD MOUNTAIN CREEK

RIVER FLOW

McCLOUD RIVER

BOUNDARY CREEK

LADY BUG CREEK

GREEN POOL CREEK

SALAMANDER CREEK

BEAR CREEK

BEETLE BUTTE CREEK

△ - CAMP

McCLOUD RIVER

5

101

70

80

580

99

McCLOUD RIVER

N

NTS

The McCloud River

This river runs cold and clear with water born from the glaciers of Mt. Shasta and the McCloud Reservoir. At times the glacial silt imbues the water column with a handsome green tint (much like you'd find in a classic steelhead stream). If you hear the McCloud's "running a bit green", grab your fly rod because the fishing can be magic! A note for the fly fishing newcomer to the McCloud: the river's quirks can be tough to learn, but once you pay your dues you'll be hooked forever!

The stream is full of stone structure. Boulders of all sizes create a playing field of pocket water, riffles and big pools. The upper river offers more habitat variety, especially small pocket water, riffles, and narrow meadow meanders. Long deep pools, tailouts and larger pockets are more characteristic of the lower river. Stream banks are typically thick with overgrown vegetation making wading techniques a key to your success. A bonus to angling on the McCloud is the wildlife in the nearby forest. It's not uncommon to find signs of black bear or wild turkey as one patrols the banks.

McCloud rainbows average 10-13" throughout the system. Occasionally fly fishers catch larger fish in the 17-20" range. If you want big trout, target the browns. Spawning browns will average 17-22". Larger, 26-30" whoppers show up every year as well.

To reach the McCloud River take Highway 5 toward the town of Mt. Shasta. Exit onto highway 89 and travel into the town of McCloud. In McCloud look for Squaw Valley Road (#11). Be patient as you follow this long winding path around Lake McCloud and eventually down to the river.

Types of Fish
Rainbow and brown trout.

Known Hatches
Spring: Golden Stone, March Brown.
June: Green Drake.
July-Aug: Ltl. Yellow Stone, Pale Evening Dun.
Fall: October Caddis, Sculpins and trout fry.
All Season: Misc. Caddis, Blue Winged Olive, Hoppers & other terrestrials.

Equipment to Use
Rods: 5 - 7 weight, 8 to 9'.
Reels: Mechanical or palm drag with 50 yds. backing.
Lines: Floating for main stream. Hi-speed, Hi-D sink-tip for fast flows or deep presentations. For deepwater streamers use #4 uniform sink line, or 130-200 grain shooting head.
Leaders: 1x to 6x, 7-12'.
Wading: Chest-high neoprenes, boots, cleats and wading staff.

Flies to Use
Nymphs: Bird's Nest #10-16, Hare's Ear #10-16, Hunched Back Infrequens "H.B.I." #14-16, Poxyback Golden Stone #6-8, Poxyback PMD & Green Drake #16, Black or Olive Poxyquill #14-18, Black AP #12-14, October Caddis Emerger #6-8, Caddis, Pheasant Tail, Prince #12-16, Dark Stonefly, Black rubber Legs, Kaufman Stone #4-8.

Streamers: Chartreuse & White Thunder Creek Marabou #2-6, Olive Matuka Sculpin #2-6, Wooly Bugger #2-10 assorted colors, Muddler Minnow #2-8, Zonker #2-6, Matuka, Leech #2-4.

Dry: Light Cahill, Parachute Adams, Parachute Hare's Ear #14-18, Elk Hair Caddis #12-16, Orange, Yellow or Gold Stimulator #8, Dave's Hopper #8-10, Yellow or Red Humpy #12-16, Black Ant #12-14.

When to Fish
May - July and October - November 15th is prime time. November is best for big brown trout fishing. Afternoon evening is generally the best time of day to fish.

Season & Limits
Open the last Saturday in April through November 15th. Restrictions on tackle and harvest vary by stream location. Generally: McCloud Dam downstream to Ladybug Creek: artificial lures with barbless hooks, 2 trout limit. Ladybug Creek downstream to lower boundary of US Forest Service loop: artificials/barbless, 0 trout. US Forest Service loop downstream to the McCloud River Club: closed all year. Refer to the DFG booklet for current rulings.

Accommodations & Services
Lodging and supplies in McCloud or Shasta. Camping is best at Fowler's Camp and Ah-Di-Na Campground.

Rating
One of Northern California's top streams, a 9.

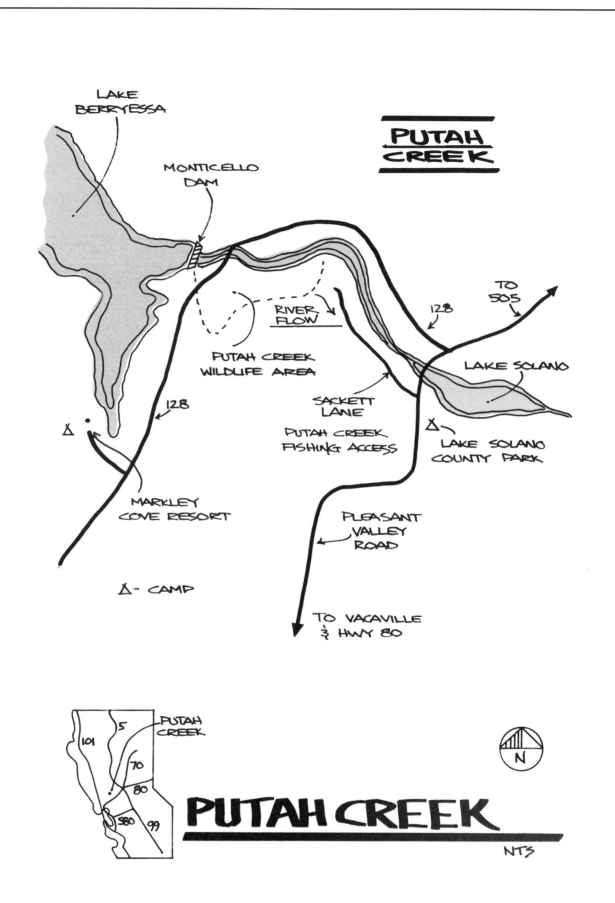

LAKE BERRYESSA

MONTICELLO DAM

PUTAH CREEK

RIVER FLOW

PUTAH CREEK WILDLIFE AREA

TO 505

128

LAKE SOLANO

SACKETT LANE

PUTAH CREEK FISHING ACCESS

LAKE SOLANO COUNTY PARK

128

MARKLEY COVE RESORT

PLEASANT VALLEY ROAD

Δ - CAMP

TO VACAVILLE & HWY 80

101 5 PUTAH CREEK

70

80

580 99

N

PUTAH CREEK

NTS

Putah Creek

If you're looking for a stream to work when the rest of the state is closed, head to Putah Creek. It's one of the few stream corridors available all year long. It's close to just about everyone in the Bay Area: under two hours from most metropolitan areas.

The main drawbacks are the shortness of the waterway and the fact that just a few miles of the stream are productive. It can be elbow-to-elbow when the bite is hot.

Putah spills out of Lake Berryessa and is a classic tailwater fishery. More often than not it runs off-colored and clarity is marginal. It's pools, riffles, runs are paralleled by brushy banks.

There's a healthy population of wild fish in the river and it's not unheard of to catch an 18-20" (or larger) fish here. Keep in mind they're winter spawners, so tread lightly as you wade during the cold season. In addition to these wild fish the Department of Fish & Game plants trout every year. Nymphing tactics are the most productive approach. The dry fly hatch is sporadic and light.

The Vacaville area is your southern approach to Putah when heading east on Highway 80. Take the Pleasant Valley Road exit directly to the river. Use Sackett Lane for streamside access. If you're coming from the north on Highway 5, Dunnigan will be your gateway. Exit onto Highway 505 and continue toward Winters. Highway 128 will take you to the water.

Types of Fish
Rainbow trout.

Known Hatches
All year: Midge, caddis, small worms and scuds.

Equipment to Use
Rods: 5 - 6 weight, 8 - 9'.
Reels: Mechanical or palm drag with at least 50 yds. backing.
Lines: Floating. Sink-tips will help with faster flows or deeper presentations.
Leaders: 4x to 6x. 6 - 9'.
Wading: Chest-high waders, studded boots. Wading staff is required. Lots of mossy rocks!

Flies to Use
Nymphs.: Bird's Nest #12-18, Hare's Ear #12-18, Prince #14-16, Poxyback PMD #16-18, Black AP #14 -18, PT Nymph #12-18, Scuds #16, Red San Juan Worm #14.

Streamers: Wooly Bugger #2-10.

Dry: Parachute Adams #14-18, Parachute Hare's Ear #14-18, Elk Hair Caddis #12-16.

When to Fish
All year.

Seasons & Limits
Special regulations apply. Last Saturday in April through November 15: 5 trout. November 16 through the Friday preceding the last Saturday in April: 0 trout. Artificial flies with barbless hooks only.

Nearby Fishing
Lake Solano and Berryessa.

Accommodations &Services
Camping and supplies at Markley Cove Resort and Lake Solano County Park.

Rating
A nearby creek and a good location for developing nymphing techniques, a 6.5.

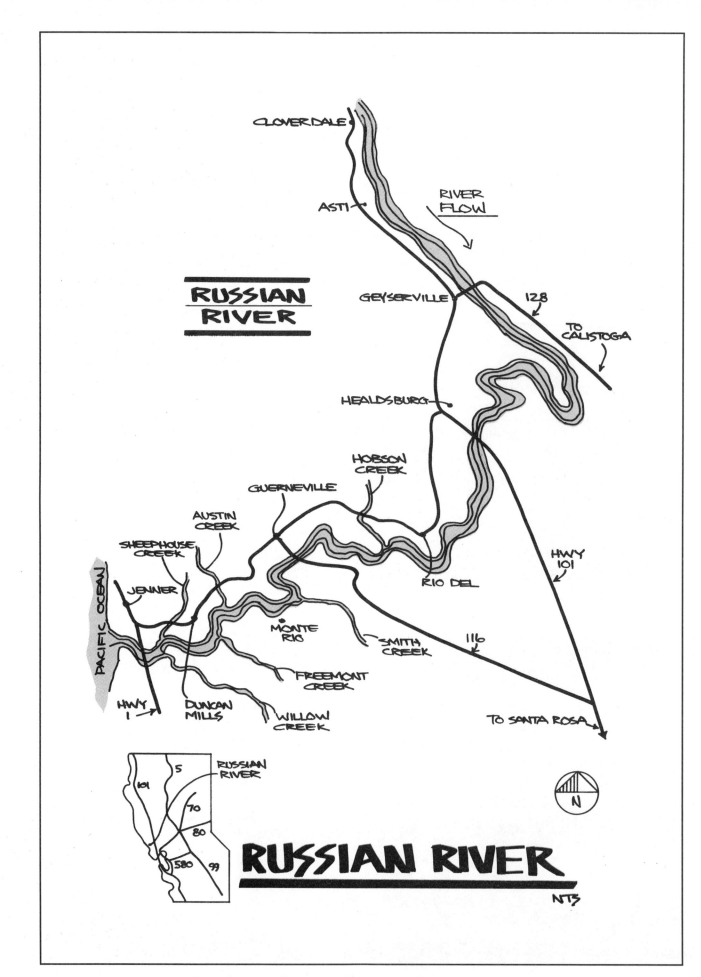

RUSSIAN RIVER

RUSSIAN RIVER

NTS

The Russian River

Of Northern California's major coastal rivers, the Russian is closest to our major population areas. It also runs through more civilization than most rivers of this type. Access is the biggest hurdle anglers contend with on the Russian River. Private lands make getting to the water difficult for anyone on foot.

The flip side to this coin is the easy wading in much of the stream, when you do find passage to the water. Deeper pools and riffles exist along the lower stretch, while the upper reaches are a mix of rapids, undercut banks, flats, and pools. In the lower region, Duncan Mills provides classic fly fishing water. Foot access increases around, and above, the town of Healdsburg.

The upper and lower sections are easily navigated with a canoe or small craft. During the fall run, most flyfishers work from prams, or skiffs, when they concentrate on fish in the tidal basin. This area is subject to low flow closures. Your success depends on the sand bar opening at the river's mouth. Contact King's Sport & Tackle [(707) 875-3483] for daily fishing conditions.

Looking for a quiet bass stream? Largemouth patrol the lower pools, while Smallmouth opportunities are best upstream in the Alexander Valley region. Since many consider the river's salmon and steelhead to be the "glory fish", the bass populations rarely receive as much pressure.

You can explore this historic waterway by driving Highway 1 along the coast to Jenner. 116 East will follow the river into Healdsburg. For inland Highway access, take 101 past Santa Rosa. 116 West will take you directly to the lower reaches. Upper-river access is possible from Highway 101 into Healdsburg, Geyserville, Asti and Cloverdale. Local surface roads take one to the river's edge.

Types of Fish
King salmon (Chinook), steelhead, shad, Smallmouth and Largemouth bass.

When to Fish
Salmon: September and October.
Steelhead: Lower river, November. Upper river, late-November to February.
Shad: May - June
Bass: All year, prime time is from late-spring to mid-fall.

Equipment to Use
Rods: 6-8 weight, 8 to 10'.
Reels: Mechanical or palm drag with 75 yards of backing.
Lines: Full floating or sink-tip lines.
Leaders: 5x to 1x, 6 - 12'.
Wading: Chest-high waders, felt-soled boots. Wading staff is recommended.

Flies to Use
Streamers: Polar Shrimp, Brindle Bug, Silver Hilton #6-10, Boss #4-10, Gold Comet #6, Glo Bugs #4-8, Muddler Minnow #6, Softshell Crayfish #8, various hot colored, bead-eye shad patterns #6.

Nymphs: Dragonfly #6, Zug Bug #10, Prince Nymph #10-12, Black A.P. #10-14, Rubber legs #4-6.

Dries: Olive Gaines Popper #8, Yellow Humpy #10-12, Dave's Hopper #8-10.

Season & Limits
Special regulations apply. Please consult the California Department of Fish & Game booklet.

Accommodations & Services
Lodging, gas, groceries and some fly fishing supplies in Jenner, Duncan Mills, Monte Rio, Guerneville, Healdsburg, and Cloverdale. Camping is best at Armstrong Redwoods State Preserve.

Rating
If the rain and water flows are consistent and the fish get past the sea lions, it could be better angling, but for now, a 5.5.

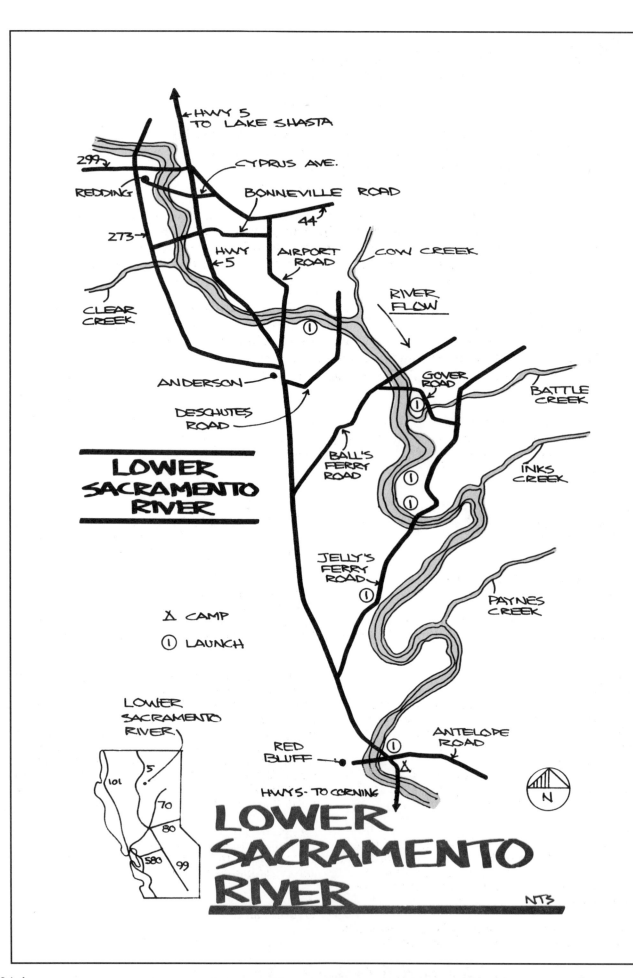

HWY 5
TO LAKE SHASTA

299

CYPRUS AVE.

REDDING

BONNEVILLE ROAD

44

273

AIRPORT ROAD

COW CREEK

HWY 5

RIVER FLOW

CLEAR CREEK

GOVER ROAD

BATTLE CREEK

ANDERSON

DESCHUTES ROAD

BALL'S FERRY ROAD

INKS CREEK

LOWER SACRAMENTO RIVER

JELLY'S FERRY ROAD

PAYNES CREEK

Δ CAMP

① LAUNCH

LOWER SACRAMENTO RIVER

5
101
70
80
580   99

RED BLUFF

ANTELOPE ROAD

HWY 5 TO CORNING

LOWER SACRAMENTO RIVER

NTS

N

The Sacramento River
Lower River

The fly fishing community recognizes "the Sac" from Lake Shasta to Sacramento as the "lower river." In this section, we target the prime territory from Redding to Red Bluff. This stretch offers big water and big fish. The wide and sweeping river runs over huge gravel bars and shallow riffles and through deep pools.

Flows are affected by weather and controlled releases. Typically the water runs around 2800 (cfs) cubic feet per second, but can be boosted well over 10,000 cfs during the summer season. Call ahead to the Bureau of Reclamation (24 hour recording 916-275-9782) to see if it's worth making the trip. High, roaring waters usually make the "fly game" a real tough proposition. Most guides say flows from 3,000 to 7,000 cfs are fishable.

Now good news. Caddis hatches on this river are incredible. Clouds of insects take flight throughout the midday hours. Dry fly action can be tremendous. Nymphing the riffles is a solid approach during non-hatch periods. Salmon begin to run the river in the fall and steelhead are right behind. For salmon use bright colored streamers, in fact some of your shad flies will work just fine for this application. For steelies try egg patterns and streamers (see below).

Reach the "Lower Sac" by driving north or south on Highway 5. At either Redding or Red Bluff, take surface roads directly to the river's edge. As a gauge for highway travel, San Francisco to Redding is around 220 miles. From the Oregon border to Redding is approximately 120 miles.

Types of Fish
King salmon (Chinook), steelhead, rainbow trout, shad and striped bass.

Known Hatches
All year: Caddis (Hydropsyche & Brachycentrus) time is March-May.
Spring & Fall: Caddis.
Summer: Midge, Little Yellow Stone, Caddis.
September-October: Mayfly (Baetis), October Caddis.

Equipment to Use
Rods: 5 - 7 weight, 8 1/2 -10'.
Reels: Mechanical drag with lots of backing.
Lines: Floating. For fast, deep water use Hi-speed, Hi-D sink tip, #4 sinking line or 130 - 200 grain shooting head.
Leaders: 0x to 7x, 6-12'.
Wading: This big river is best fished from a boat. Otherwise, use chest-high neoprene waders, felt-soled boots and wading staff.

Flies to Use
Nymphs: Bird's Nest, Beadhead & Prince, Beadhead PT, Zug Bug, Sparkle Emergent Pupa, Pulsator Caddis #12-14, Hare's Ear #10-16, Z-Wing Caddis Emerger #12-16, Hunch Back Infrequens #18.

Streamers: various color Woolly Bugger, Muddler Minnow #2-10, various color Shad Fly #6.

Drys Elk Hair Caddis, Yellow Humpy #12-16, Black Ant #12-14, Parachute Adams, Parachute Hare's Ear #14-18, Burk's CDC Stone #14, X Caddis #14-16, Glo Bug #6-8.

When to Fish
Rainbow: March-Nov, prime time is March/April & Oct.
Steelhead: Sept.-March, prime time is Jan-March.
Shad: May-August, prime time is June and July.

Seasons & Limits
Restrictions on tackle and harvest apply. 650 feet below the Keswick Dam to the Deschutes Road bridge: Barbless hooks only, 1 trout, 0 salmon in possession. Deschutes Road bridge to Bend bridge: Aug.1 - Jan.14, 3 trout, 2 salmon. Jan.15 - Jul. 31, 3 trout, 0 salmon. From September 1 through February 28, no rainbow trout or steelhead over 22 inches may be possessed in the waters identified here. It's best to refer to current regulations before heading to the river.

Accommodations & Services
Lodging and supplies in Redding or Red Bluff. Camping in the Red Bluff area. Eight launch ramps, some with fee.

Rating
Overall, an 8.5.

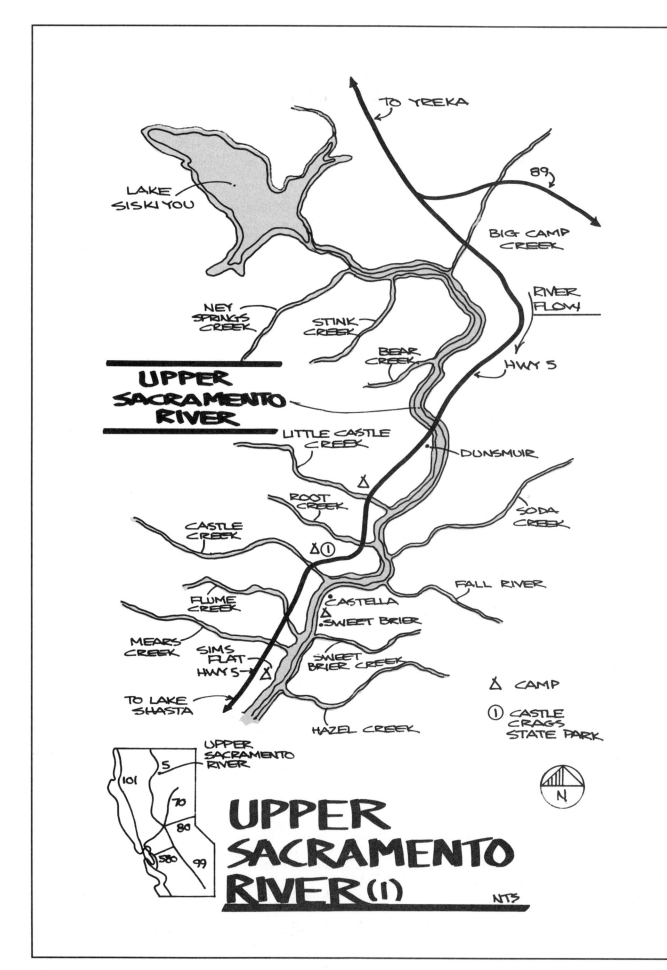

TO YREKA

89

LAKE SISKIYOU

BIG CAMP CREEK

NEY SPRINGS CREEK

STINK CREEK

BEAR CREEK

RIVER FLOW

UPPER SACRAMENTO RIVER

HWY 5

LITTLE CASTLE CREEK

DUNSMUIR

ROOT CREEK

SODA CREEK

CASTLE CREEK

FALL RIVER

FLUME CREEK

CASTELLA

SWEET BRIER

MEARS CREEK

SIMS FLAT HWY 5

SWEET BRIER CREEK

TO LAKE SHASTA

HAZEL CREEK

△ CAMP

① CASTLE CRAGS STATE PARK

UPPER SACRAMENTO RIVER

5
101
70
80
580
99

N

UPPER SACRAMENTO RIVER (I)

NTS

The Sacramento River
Upper River

This section, the "Grand Daddy" of Northern California fly fishing rivers, is gorgeous in all respects. It provides fly fishers a Class-A experience most anytime they explore this outstanding fishery.

Amazingly, we almost lost "The Sac" on July 14th, 1991. A railroad tanker car crashed and spilled some 19,000 gallons of herbicide into the stream. Nearly all the fish died. I believe it was one of the largest environmental disasters in the West.

Mother Nature, however, is incredible. From the sliver of life that remained in the stream, the Upper Sac rebuilt itself. Nature's work (and some creative fishery management) has resulted in a revitalized food chain for wild trout and smallmouth bass. This is perhaps the best application of the popular phrase "It's baaaaaaaaaccccckk!".

The uppermost section (above Sims) has classic pocket water. The trout here are consistently larger than before the spill. Ted Fay, a legend in these parts, was responsible for popularizing the "two fly", short-line nymphing technique that is so successful. Ask at a nearby fly shop if you've questions about this set up.

Walk the lower stretch (below Sims to the La Moine area) and you'll find a mixture of trout and aggressive smallmouth bass. I stress *walk* by the way. Most anglers stay near the parking areas. Take the time to hike a short distance down the train tracks and you'll usually find uncrowded waters (do keep an eye out for trains). Anywhere you fish the Upper Sac you'll find easy access. The Interstate and many surface roads run right next to or near the river.

Interstate highway 5 is the state's central artery and THE way, north or south, to the river. Nearly any exit provides stream side access, but be prepared for some unimproved dirt roads. Parking areas are generally small, so be flexible.

Types of Fish
Rainbow and Brown trout and some Smallmouth bass.

Known Hatches
May-June: Little Yellow & Golden Stone, Green Drake.
October - November: October Caddis, Midge.
All year: Caddis, particularly Hydropsychids and Rhyacophilids, Pale Morning and Pale Evening Duns.

Equipment to Use
Rods: 4-6 weight, 8 - 10'.
Reels: Standard mechanical or palm drag.
Lines: Floating. Hi-speed, Hi-D sink-tip, sinking, shooting tapers.
Leaders: 6x to 3x, 6 - 12' or more.
Wading: Chest-high neoprene waders, studded boots and wading staff.

Flies to Use
Nymphs: Bird's Nest #14-16, Hare's Ear, Pheasant Tail #12-16, Hunchback Infrequens "H.B.I." #14-18, Poxyback PMD #16, Black AP #12-14, Oct. Caddis Emerger #6-8, Poxyquill #18-20, Poxyback Golden Stone #10, Poxyback Green Drake #12.

Streamers: Olive/White Marabou Thunder Creek, Olive Matuka Sculpin #2-6, assorted colors of Wooly Bugger #2-10, Muddler Minnow #2-8.

Drys: Light Cahill, Parachute Adams, Parachute Hare's Ear, Elk Hair Caddis, Royal Trude, X Caddis.#14-16., Orange or Gold Stimulator, Chartreuse Gaines Popper #8, Dave's Hopper #8-10, Yellow or Orange Humpy #12-16, Black Ant #12-14.

When to Fish
May and mid-September through mid-November are the best, though there's action of some kind all season on this river!

Seasons & Limits
River management is changeable here. Consult the DF&G regulations, or ask at a nearby fly shop. Generally, fish from the last Saturday in April through November 15, artificials and barbless hooks only. Box Canyon Dam down to Scarlet Way Bridge: 0 trout. Scarlet Way downstream to Soda Creek: 5 per day, 10 in possession. Soda Creek downstream to Shasta Lake: 0 trout.

Accommodations & Services
Lodging and supplies in Dunsmuir, Castella, Lakehead and the town of Mount Shasta. Camping is good at Castle Crags State Park, Railroad Park and Sims Flat.

Rating
Near a major highway, pretty, not too crowded, plenty of great fly fishing water, a 9.

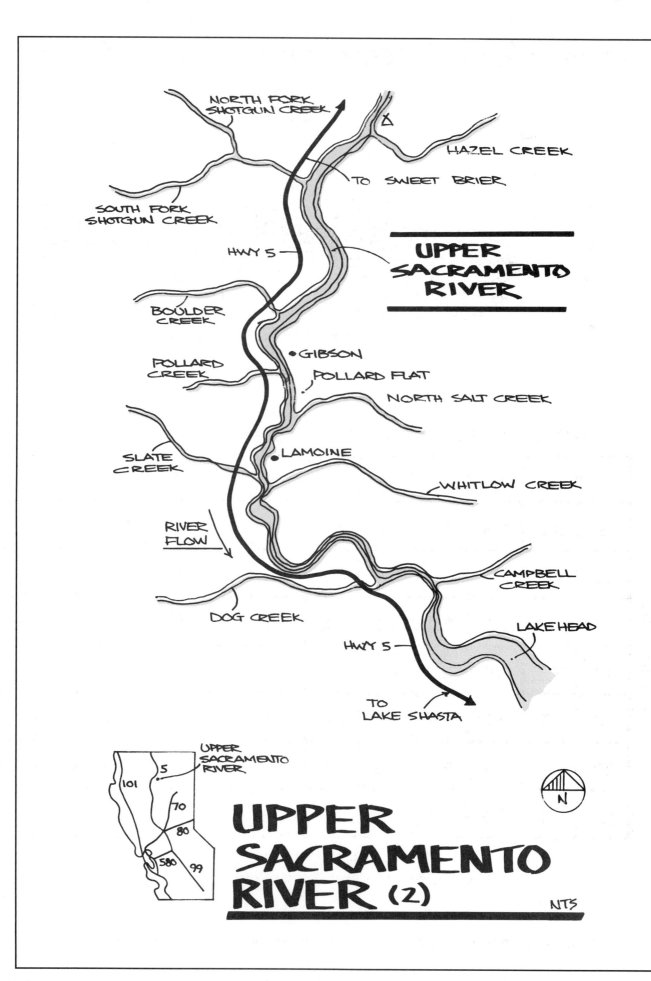

NORTH FORK
SHOTGUN CREEK

HAZEL CREEK

TO SWEET BRIER

SOUTH FORK
SHOTGUN CREEK

UPPER
SACRAMENTO
RIVER

HWY 5

BOULDER
CREEK

POLLARD
CREEK

• GIBSON

POLLARD FLAT

NORTH SALT CREEK

SLATE
CREEK

• LAMOINE

WHITLOW CREEK

RIVER
FLOW

CAMPBELL
CREEK

DOG CREEK

LAKEHEAD

HWY 5

TO
LAKE SHASTA

UPPER
SACRAMENTO
RIVER

101

5

70

80

580

99

UPPER
SACRAMENTO
RIVER (2)

N

NTS

Weigh Your Catch With a Tape Measure

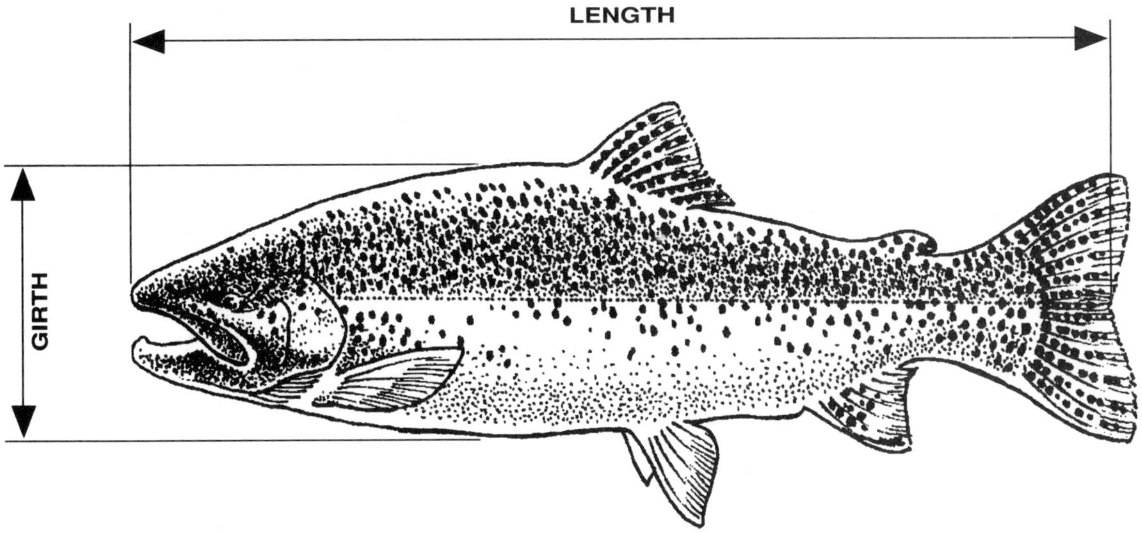

***EXAMPLE:** A fish 20" long and 14" around (at its thickest part) weighs 4.9 lbs.*

Girth (inches)	10	12	14	16	18	20	22	24	26	28	30
8	0.8	1.0	1.1	1.3	1.4	1.6	1.8	1.9	2.1	2.2	2.4
10	1.3	1.5	1.8	2.0	2.3	2.5	2.8	3.0	3.3	3.5	3.8
12	1.8	2.2	2.5	2.9	3.2	3.6	4.0	4.3	4.7	5.0	5.4
14	2.5	2.9	3.4	3.9	4.4	4.9	5.4	5.9	6.4	6.9	7.4
16	3.2	3.8	4.5	5.1	5.8	6.4	7.0	7.7	8.3	9.0	9.6
18	4.1	4.9	5.7	6.5	7.3	8.1	8.9	9.7	10.5	11.3	12.2
20	5.0	6.0	7.0	8.0	9.0	10.0	11.0	12.0	13.0	14.0	15.0

Length (inches)
Tip of nose to notch at the center of tail.

Courtesy of Ralph & Lisa Cutter's California School of Flyfishing • P.O. Box 8212, Truckee, CA 96162 • 1 (800) 58-TROUT

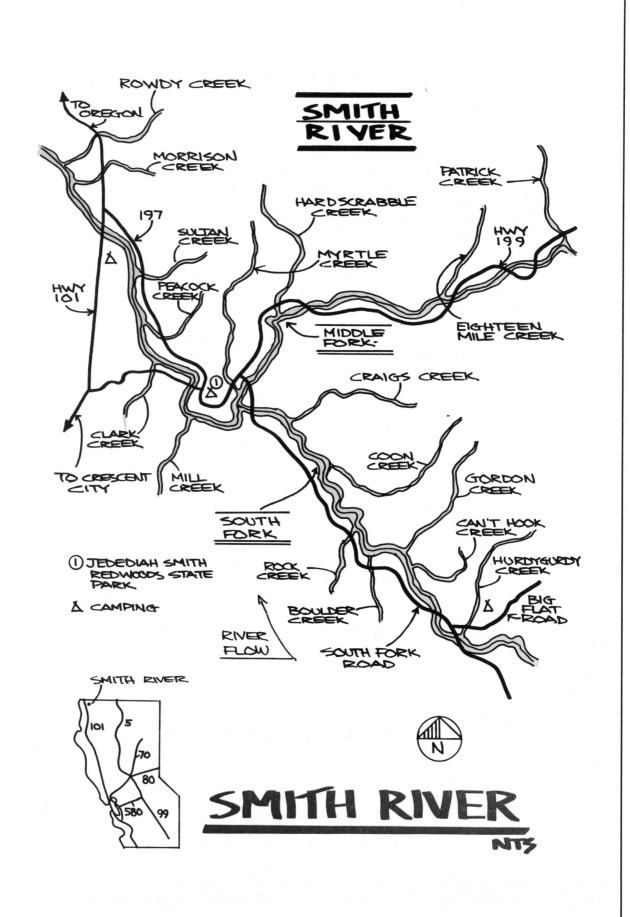

SMITH RIVER

ROWDY CREEK

TO OREGON

MORRISON CREEK

197

SULTAN CREEK

HARDSCRABBLE CREEK

PATRICK CREEK

HWY 199

MYRTLE CREEK

PEACOCK CREEK

HWY 101

MIDDLE FORK

EIGHTEEN MILE CREEK

CRAIGS CREEK

CLARK CREEK

COON CREEK

GORDON CREEK

TO CRESCENT CITY

MILL CREEK

CAN'T HOOK CREEK

SOUTH FORK

HURDYGURDY CREEK

① JEDEDIAH SMITH REDWOODS STATE PARK

ROCK CREEK

BIG FLAT ROAD

Δ CAMPING

BOULDER CREEK

SOUTH FORK ROAD

RIVER FLOW

SMITH RIVER

101   5

70

80

580   99

N

SMITH RIVER

NTS

The Smith River

This is a glorious fishery with much to offer. The long drive will be worth it. The streams' wild nature and the beauty of the surrounding territory combine to make a perfect setting for your angling adventure.

The Smith has held the state record for steelhead for some time. It tipped the scales at over 27 pounds. We're talking large steelies here, averaging 12-18 pounds every year. If salmon is your game, look no further. The Smith is home to world-class Kings running 20-50 lbs. Even larger fish can excite the lucky angler in the right place, at the right time. Nothing comes easy on the Smith, however. Expect to make many presentations. Expect to go fishless more often than not. Yet when everything comes together, expect high quality steelhead and salmon to go after your fly.

Being the northern most coastal fishery in our state, weather (wind, rain, mud, etc.) can be a real factor when it comes to stream access. One of the pluses of this fishery is its ability to clear itself extremely quickly after a storm. This makes it one of the most fly rod friendly streams in the winter.

The river is best explored from a drift boat. Bank access is limited. Chinook action is best during the early fall season, while the steelhead begin showing up in late fall. They continue to enter the stream through the winter months.

Often overlooked, but also fun, is the local cutthroat fishery. It's the perfect pursuit for lightline aficionados. Sea-run Cutts are found throughout the tidal basin and are catchable during the summer months. In addition, the tidal basin harbors surfperch, smelt, and flounder.

Directions to the region are simple. Take Highway 101 to Crescent City and then take 199 straight to the river. If you prefer to work the estuary environs, take 101 to Fort Dick and follow Morehead Road to Lower Lake Road.

Types of Fish
King salmon (Chinook), Steelhead, Cutthroat trout.

When to Fish
Kings: September-January, prime time is late Oct-Dec.
Steelhead: November-April, prime time is Nov-Mar.
Cutthroat trout: Summer months are best.

Known Hatches
The tidal basin is loaded with baitfish, isopods and shrimp. Upstream, dark nymphs and spawn style patterns are most effective.

Equipment to Use
Rods: 7 - 9 weight, 9 - 10'.
Reels: Mechanical and palm drag with 100 yards of backing.
Lines: Sinking shooting head system or sink-tip lines, 150 - 300 grains.
Leaders: 1x to 3x, 6 - 9'.
Wading: Chest-high neoprene waders, felt soled boots. A wading staff is a must.

Flies to Use
Streamers & Nymphs
Tidewater area: Thor #6, Screaming Shad Shrimp #4-6, Horner Deerhair Shrimp #6, various Scuds #12-14, small baitfish patterns #2-4, primary colors are silver/blue and all silver.
Main stream area: Burlap, Silver Hilton, Mossback #6-10, Boss #4-10, Glo Bugs #6.

Accommodations & Services
This is a remote area. The best camping is at Jedediah Smith Redwoods State Park. There are also a couple Forest Service campgrounds on Highway 199. Lodging is available at the Ship Ashore (Best Western) 1-800-528-1234, near the town of Gasquet and in Crescent City.

Season & Limits
This river is subject to low flow closure. Consult your current Department of Fish and Game regulations booklet for additional details.

Rating
The Smith is one of the best in the West! Outstanding fish and quality water demand high levels of fly fishing skills, a big 9.

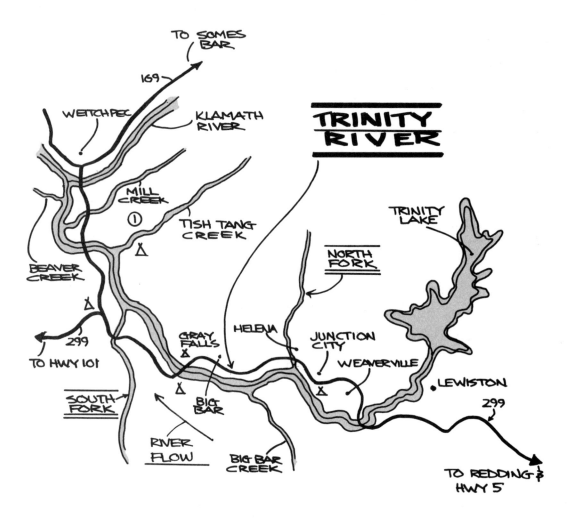

TO SOMES
BAR

169

WEITCHPEC

KLAMATH
RIVER

**TRINITY
RIVER**

MILL
CREEK

①

TISH TANG
CREEK

TRINITY
LAKE

NORTH
FORK

BEAVER
CREEK

299

TO HWY 101

GRAY
FALLS

HELENA

JUNCTION
CITY

WEAVERVILLE

LEWISTON

299

SOUTH
FORK

BIG
BAR

TO REDDING &
HWY 5

RIVER
FLOW

BIG BAR
CREEK

① HOOPA RESERVATION

⛺ CAMPING

TRINITY
RIVER

101

5

70

80

580

99

N

TRINTY RIVER

NTS

The Trinity River

The Trinity watershed is an amazing system seemingly made for the fly fisher: great trout fly fishing, superb steelhead runs, a pristine setting. Each of the river's sections are completely different, so I separate the river like this: lower region, Weitchpec to Hoopa Valley, wide-open "tidal" waters. Middle section, Willow Creek to Junction City, pools deep in the canyon. Upper reaches, Weaverville to Lewiston Dam, a small mountain stream.

This highly productive salmon and steelhead fishery is fly fishing friendly. Roads parallel many sections of the river and have many turnouts. Bank access is almost unlimited so wading anglers can enjoy all kinds of water. Hike-in fly fishing is worth the effort and the river's manageable size permits casting to nearly all holes, riffles and runs.

The river's three sections provide a thorough workout of your field techniques. The variety of habitat and feisty fish demand everything from short-line nymphing techniques to skating big dry flies on "greased-line" swings. Subtly drifting egg patterns works at times too.

The fish here typically weigh 2-12 pounds. Kings average 6-12 lbs. Silvers are generally 8 or 9 lbs., though few and far between. Steelhead, which run fall to spring, run 4 to 8 pounds. The hard-to-catch brown trout average 2-4 lbs. There are some 6-8 pounders that give one a real thrill.

Most flyfishers get to the river from Redding and Highway 299 West. To work the lower stretch, near the confluence of the Klamath River, follow Highway 96 past Hoopa and onto Weitchpec. Northcoast anglers can take Highway 101 south to Arcata, then 299 East to Willow Creek, the major Steelhead section.

Types of Fish
King salmon (Chinook), Silver salmon (Coho), Steelhead, Brown trout.

Known Hatches
Fall: Isonychia Mayfly, October Caddis, BWO.
Winter: Baetis and Pale Morning Duns, Golden Stonefly.
Salmon and fresh-run steelhead: Use streamers.
Tidal basin: Baitfish, isopods and shrimp.
Upper river Dark streamers, nymphs and spawn-style patterns.

Equipment to Use
Rods: 6-8 weight, 9 - 10'
Reels: Click or palm drag, 75+ yrds. backing.
Lines: Full floating or sink-tip lines.
Leaders: 5x to 2x, 6 - 12'.
Wading: Chest-high neoprene waders, felt-soled boots. A wading staff is recommended.

Flies to Use
Streamers: Thor, Gold Comet, Muddler Minnow #6, Burlap, Brindle Bug, Silver Hilton #6-10, Boss #4-10, Chappie #2-8, Babine Special #4-8.

Nymphs: Poxyback Isonychia PMD #10-16, Poxyback Golden Stone #6, Prince #10-12, Black A.P., Gold Ribbed Hare's Ear #10-14, Rubberlegs #4-6.

Dries: Madam X #6-8, Orange Stimulator #8, PMD Sparkle Dun #16-18, Elk Hair Caddis #10-16, Burk's Krystal Waker #4-8, Lani's Waller Waker #4, Paradun sulfur #16-20.

When to Fish
Salmon
Lower river: Summer.
Middle section: July - September.
Steelhead
Lower river: Sept. - Oct.
Middle river: November - January
Upper river: late winter.
Brown Trout
Primarily upper river: November - March.

Seasons & Limits
Rules are complicated and change rapidly on this river and there are often "special" regulations. Check your current California DFG regulations booklet and at a fly shop.

Accommodations & Services
Lodging and supplies in Hoopa, Willow Creek, Junction City and Weaverville. Camping areas and sites abound throughout the area!

Rating
Overall, a solid 7.

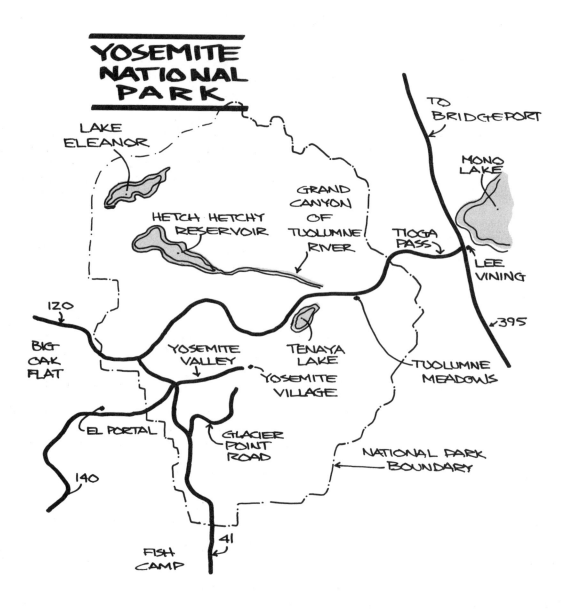

YOSEMITE NATIONAL PARK

TO BRIDGEPORT

LAKE ELEANOR

MONO LAKE

GRAND CANYON OF TUOLUMNE RIVER

HETCH HETCHY RESERVOIR

TIOGA PASS

LEE VINING

120

395

BIG OAK FLAT

YOSEMITE VALLEY

TENAYA LAKE

YOSEMITE VILLAGE

TUOLUMNE MEADOWS

EL PORTAL

GLACIER POINT ROAD

NATIONAL PARK BOUNDARY

140

41

FISH CAMP

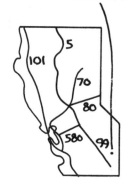

YOSEMITE NATIONAL PARK

5

101

70

80

580

99

YOSEMITE NATIONAL PARK

NTS

N

Yosemite
National Park

When considering an angling visit to Yosemite make your plans in this order: sight-seeing, hiking, camping and then fly fishing.

The high Sierra isn't a place to catch huge fish. Harsh winters and short growing seasons mean only the heartiest trout survive (average sizes 6-10"). But don't let small trout keep you away. Just getting to the waters and fly fishing in Yosemite is well worth it. The fish are exquisite examples of what high mountain trout are all about. The scenery is phenomenal and all that's needed is leg power. Use the map in this guide for general reference, DO NOT use it for hiking directions. Get and study a good topographical map of the area before you head out.

Most anglers work the stillwaters (over 100). For catching, your best bets are the old stocked trout in Tilden, Smedberg, Minnow, Wilmer, Virginia, Mattie, Edyth and Benson lakes. I believe the many back country streams present the greatest challenges and rewards. You'll need to use your "short cast" skills to negotiate most of these intimate streams.

As mentioned, fly fishing here is really an adjunct to the experience. The early explorer and champion of the area, John Muir, had it right when he called the Sierra Nevada "The Range of Light." The Yosemite portion of the range is perfect for sunrise and sunset. There's something magical in the mountains and forests of this vast country. Little more needs to be said other than, ...get out and revel in the glory of Yosemite!

There's four main entrances to the park. From the East (Highway 395) take Highway 120 at Lee Vining. From the South (Fresno) take Highway 41 to Fish Camp. From the West at Big Oak Flat take highway 120 for the direct route to Tuolumne Meadows. Travel on Highway 140 (from Highway 99) to El Portal to get right into Yosemite Valley. All roads into the park are well paved and easy to negotiate.

Types of Fish
Rainbow, brown and brook trout.

Known Hatches
May-July: Callibaetis, Pale Morning Dun, Spotted Sedge, Alderfly and Midge.
July-September: Callibaetis, Blue-Winged Olive, Trico, Pale Morning Dun, American Grannom, Spotted Sedge, Midge and Damselfly.

Equipment to Use
Rods: 4-6 weight, 7 - 9'.
Reels: Standard mechanical or palm drag.
Lines: Floating. #2 Sink-tip, helps with deep water.
Leaders: 3x to 6x, 6 - 12'.
Wading: Chest-high waders and felt-soled boots. A wading staff is recommended. Bank angling is no problem. Float tubes are a bonus for stillwaters.

Flies to Use
Nymphs: Olive Bird's Nest #12-14, Hunched Back Infrequens "H.B.I.", PT #16-20, Green Sparkle Pupa #16-18 Damselfly #10-12, Scuds #10-16, Tangerine Dream #6-8, Poxyback Callibaetis #14-16, G.R. Hare's Ear #12-16.

Streamers: Olive or Brown Wooly Buggers #8-10.

Dries: Tan or Olive Paradun #16-20, Tricos #18-20, Brown Elk Hair Caddis, Little Yellow Stone #14-16, Henryville Special #16, Goddard Caddis, Yellow Humpy #12-14, Fur Ants #10-16, Hopper #8.

When to Fish
May through November, prime time is late-June - Oct.

Seasons & Limits
Last Saturday in April to November 15th. Check the current DF&G regulations booklet or at a local fly shop.

Accommodations & Services
Lodging, camping and supplies are abundant in Yosemite Valley and Tuolumne Meadows. Check with park headquarters for reservations and information, (209) 372-0302. An entry fee is charged and special permits are necessary for travel in the back country.

Rating
Great high country, pretty little trout, overall an 8.5.

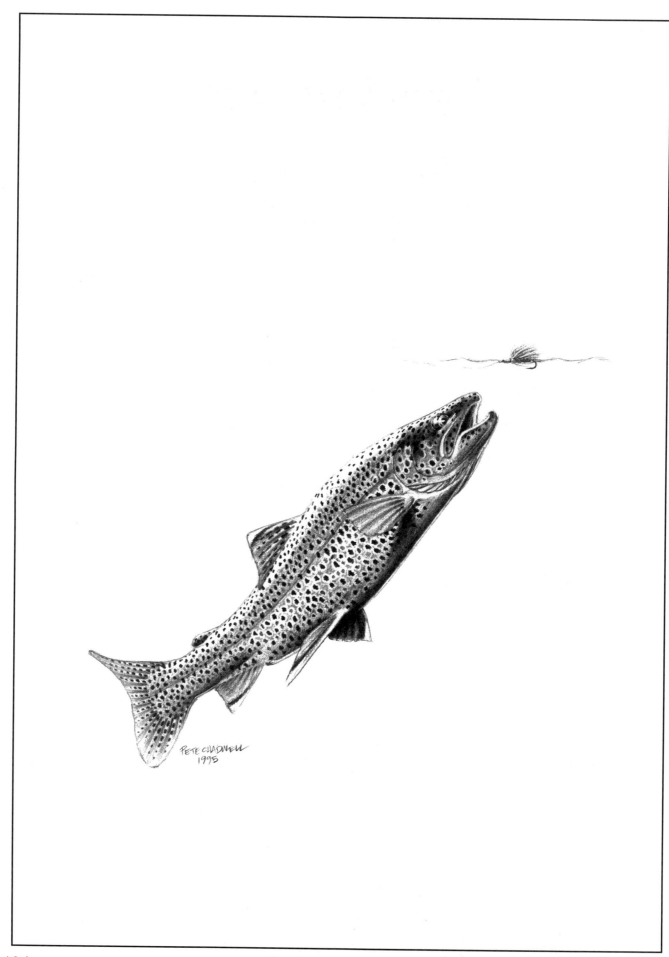

Section Two

Selected Lakes,

Reservoirs

&

Saltwater

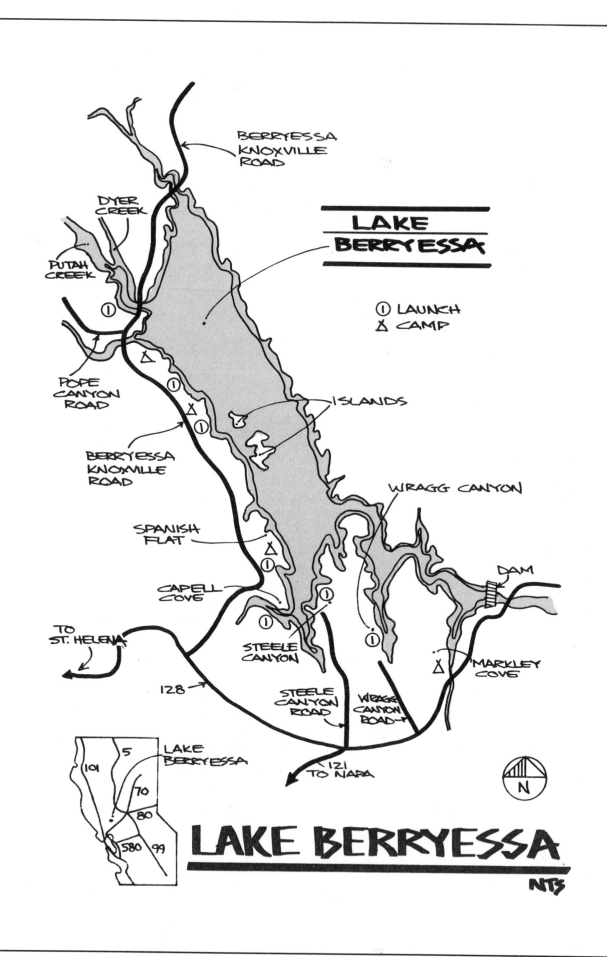

LAKE BERRYESSA

Lake Berryessa

This 25 mile lake is probably one of the most heavily used water resources in the Bay Area. But for a good reason: there's tons of fish and great fishing. It's a bass angler's dream and home of an outstanding trophy trout fishery. It's also easy to get to, scenic, has plenty of camping and services and can be a fun picnic or party spot. Hence, it can be a bit overpopulated at times. Stay sharp when you're out amidst all the boat traffic. Better yet, try to go to Berryessa midweek.

Bass in Lake Berryessa follow the classic calendar. They're active in the shallows during the spring spawning cycle and during the autumn minnow bite. They cruise brush and rocky points. Work from a float tube in the lake's southern arms especially Steele and Wragg Canyons. Smallmouth often congregate at the north end of Berryessa near Pope and Putah Creek.

Berryessa is stocked with over 100,000 trout each year. They run from 10 - 20" and go down deep during the summer months. Try deep water streamer tactics at around 20 to 30 feet. In autumn the lake "turns over" and trout are closer to the surface and within easy range of most line designs.

Throughout the year Berryessa plays host to many fishing tournaments. To avoid this competition contact one of the lake's resorts or the Lake Berryessa Visitor Information line (707/966-2111). The lake is 50 miles west of Sacramento and 65 miles north of San Francisco.

Types of Fish
Rainbow and brown trout, largemouth, smallmouth and spotted bass, crappie, bluegill and catfish.

When to Fish
Bass: March - November, prime time is Apr-May & Oct-Nov.
Trout: Fall and winter, prime time is Oct and early Nov.
Crappie: Spring and summer.

Known Baitfish
For bass, "Dads-n-Shad" plus worms, grubs and frogs. For trout, imitate small baitfish.

Equipment to Use
Rods: 6 - 9 weight, 8 1/2 - 10'.
Reels: Palm or mechanical drag.
Lines: Intermediate sink or heavy sink shooting head. Floating for poppers.
Leaders: 1x to 4x, 7 - 12'.
Wading: A terrific lake for float tubes and prams. OK bank angling.

Flies to Use
Streamers: Blanton's Flash Tail series #2-8, Zonker #6, Jansen's Threadfin Shad #6, Purple Eelworm #6, Burk's V-Worm #10, Whitlock Softshell Crayfish #8, Poxybou Crayfish #4-8, Black Woolly Bugger #4, Black Hare Jig #6.

Topwater: Swimming Frog #6, Whitlock's Red Head Hair Popper #6, Deerhair Mouse #4, Chartreuse Diver #4.

Accommodations & Services
This place has it all: seven full-service resorts and marinas with ramps and campsites galore. It's a great lake for a houseboat expedition too.

Seasons & Limits
One can fish for something just about any time of the year. Check current California fishing regulations or at one of the fly shops or marinas for specific information.

Rating
For convenience, proximity and quality fish a 9.

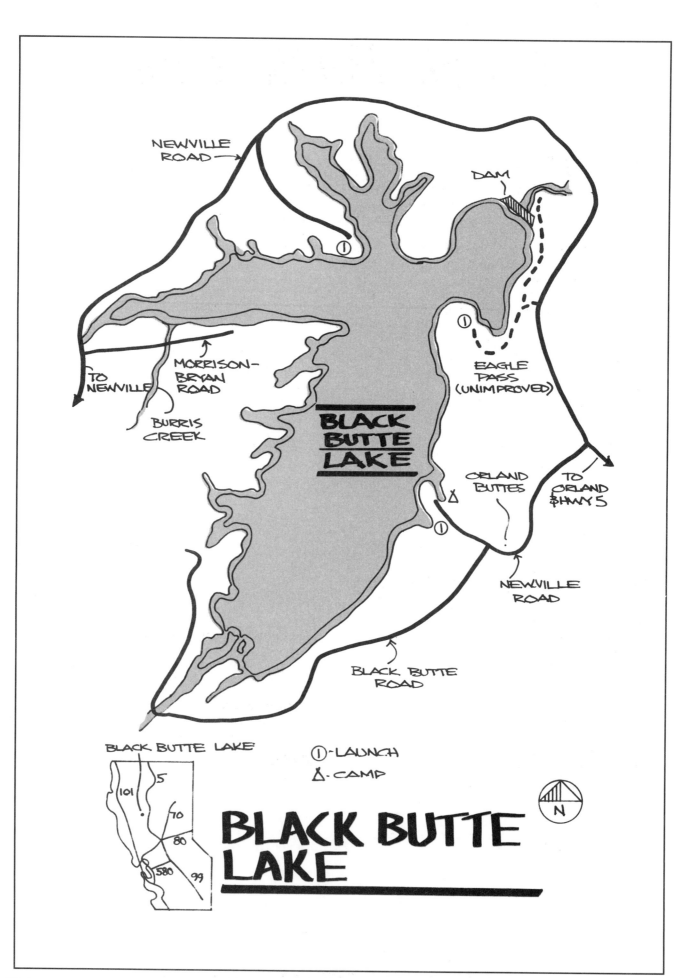

NEWVILLE ROAD

DAM

TO NEWVILLE

MORRISON-BRYAN ROAD

BURRIS CREEK

BLACK BUTTE LAKE

EAGLE PASS (UNIMPROVED)

ORLAND BUTTES

TO ORLAND &HWY 5

NEWVILLE ROAD

BLACK BUTTE ROAD

BLACK BUTTE LAKE

Ⓘ-LAUNCH

△-CAMP

101
5
70
80
580
99

BLACK BUTTE LAKE

N

Black Butte Lake

This popular lake provides a cool place for outdoor recreation in the warm months and a fine warm water fly fishing destination during the cooler months. There are 3 boat ramps and some 40 miles of shoreline. All this plus adequate shoreline facilities and an easy 12 miles off the Interstate Highway 5 corridor (at Orland) combine to make a good fly rodding destination.

This Army Corps of Engineers reservoir is best known for its spring crappie fishing, perhaps the best in the state. These fish grow to 2 pounds or more. Largemouth bass up to 6 pound are also popular here. The small protected coves on the western shore provide the most consistent action. Stumps, rocky cover and tapering points of land are the best features to look for when fly fishing Black Butte.

The black bass populations fluctuate and get hit hard during the peak months in spring. Summer weather can sometimes be like a blast furnace here. When it gets into the 100's, the fishing gets tough and the boat traffic is significant. This is a great time to try for catfish or head elsewhere. Expect to see many people here in the summer or on nice weather days. You can do quite well if you target the cooler months for a fly fishing trip to Black Butte Lake.

To get to Black Butte Lake, take I - 5 to the farming town of Orland, about 40 miles south of Red Bluff. Exit west on Black Butte Lake road. Then go 12 miles on Newville road.

Types of Fish
Largemouth bass, crappie, bluegill and catfish.

When to Fish
Bass: All year, prime time is spring.
Panfish, especially crappie: spring & fall.

Known Baitfish
Crawdads and minnows.

Equipment to Use
Rods: 5 - 7 weight, 8 1/2 - 9'.
Reels: Palm or mechanical drag.
Lines: Floating, intermediate, or sink-tip type 3.
Leaders: 1x to 5x, 5 -.9'.
Wading: Hip boots for fishing from the bank. Use a float tube for fishing along the shore and in coves.

Flies to Use
Streamers: Zonker #6, Burk's V-Worms #10, Whitlock Softshell Crayfish #8, Poxybou Crayfish #4-8.

Nymphs: Jansen Callibaetis, Zug Bug #14, PT #16.

Topwater: Deer hair Mouse #6, Dave's Hopper #6, Gaines Micro Poppers #8-10.

Accommodations & Services
Three launch ramps, a supply store, marina, boat rentals and a variety of campsites. Lodging and gas are available in Orland.

Seasons & Limits
General season, consult the California Department of Fish and game regulations booklet.

Rating
Boats and hot water can put the fish down, otherwise, a 6.

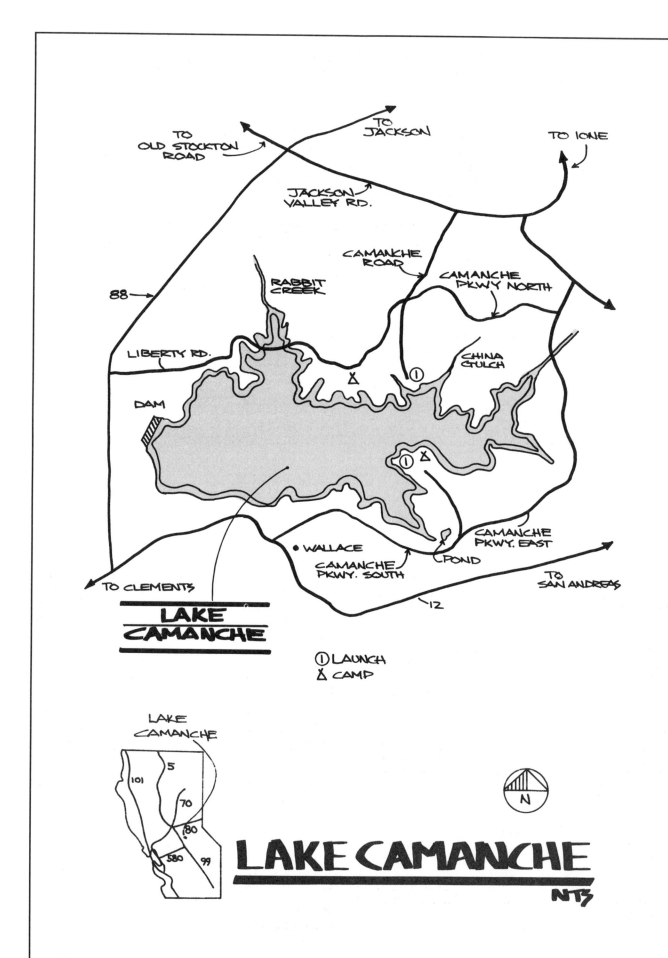

TO OLD STOCKTON ROAD

TO JACKSON

TO IONE

JACKSON VALLEY RD.

CAMANCHE ROAD

CAMANCHE PKWY NORTH

RABBIT CREEK

88

CHINA GULCH

LIBERTY RD.

DAM

CAMANCHE PKWY. EAST

• WALLACE

POND

CAMANCHE PKWY. SOUTH

TO CLEMENTS

TO SAN ANDREAS

12

LAKE CAMANCHE

Ⓘ LAUNCH
△ CAMP

LAKE CAMANCHE

101
5
70
80
580
99

N

LAKE CAMANCHE
NTS

Lake Camanche

Located in the heart of the Sierra Nevada foothill's Mother Load Country, this full service reservoir provides some of the best early season fishing in the area. There are approximately 60 miles of shore, rocky shore, points and coves. When the lake is full there are over 7,500 surface acres of water. When the weather is very warm many of these acres are taken by waterskiers.

Fortunately for the fly fisher, the better fishing is during the cooler weather of spring. All varieties of fish are available. To catch the warm water species try a crawdad color scheme with red, brown, blue and orange. Anything that slithers or crawls through "bassy" cover is sure to draw fish. For the stocked trout and kokanee, fish down about 10 to 20 feet or to the 50 - 55° temperate zone. Bank angling is best around the south and north shores.

If topwater is your game, fish in the early morning or evening time slots. When the summer sun is beating down, most all the gamefish go deep, 30 feet or more. Deep water streamer tactics will keep you in the game. Night fishing for crappie is usually productive.

Camanche is east of the Central valley city of Stockton about 30 miles. Drive east on Highway 88 to Clements. From here it's east on Liberty Road for north shore access or six miles on Highway 12 to reach the south shore.

Types of Fish
Rainbow trout, kokanee salmon, spotted, smallmouth and largemouth bass, crappie and bluegill.

When to Fish
Trout: November - April, prime time is Jan-Apr.
Bass: March - November, prime time is Apr-May and Oct-Nov.
Panfish: All year, prime time is spring and summer.

Known Hatches
Trout key on Callibaetis mayflies, tan or yellow Caddis, damselfly nymphs and shad streamers. Bass dine primarily on crawdads. For panfish use small jigs, nymphs and sponge spiders.

Equipment to Use
Rods: 5 - 7 weight, 8 1/2 - 10'.
Reels: Palm or mechanical drag.
Lines: Intermediate, or heavy sink shooting head.
Leaders: 2x to 4x, 6 - 12'.
Wading: Best to work the lake from a boat or float tube. From shore, hip boots are OK, neoprene and felt-soled boots are warmer.

Flies to Use
Streamers: Purple Eelworm #6, Purple or Brown V-Worm #10, Poxybou Crayfish #4-8, Black Woolly Bugger #4, Bullet Head #6, Blanton's Flash Tail Series #6-8, Whitlock's Near Nuff Sculpin #6.

Nymphs: Poxyback Callibaetis #16, Black Ant #14, Gold Bead Prince Nymph #10-16, Bug Eye Damsel #12.

Topwater: Bett's Bull-it Frog #1/0, Andy's Loudmouth Shad #6, Gaines Micro Popper #8-10, Elk Hair Caddis #10, Sponge Spiders #10-12.

Accommodations & Services
Camping, public launches, marina, boat rentals, store and supplies are available at the lake.

Seasons & Limits
Fish all year and plan on general state regulations. Check at a fly shop, the Camanche store or consult the California DF&G regulation booklet for more exact information.

Rating
Overall a 6.5.

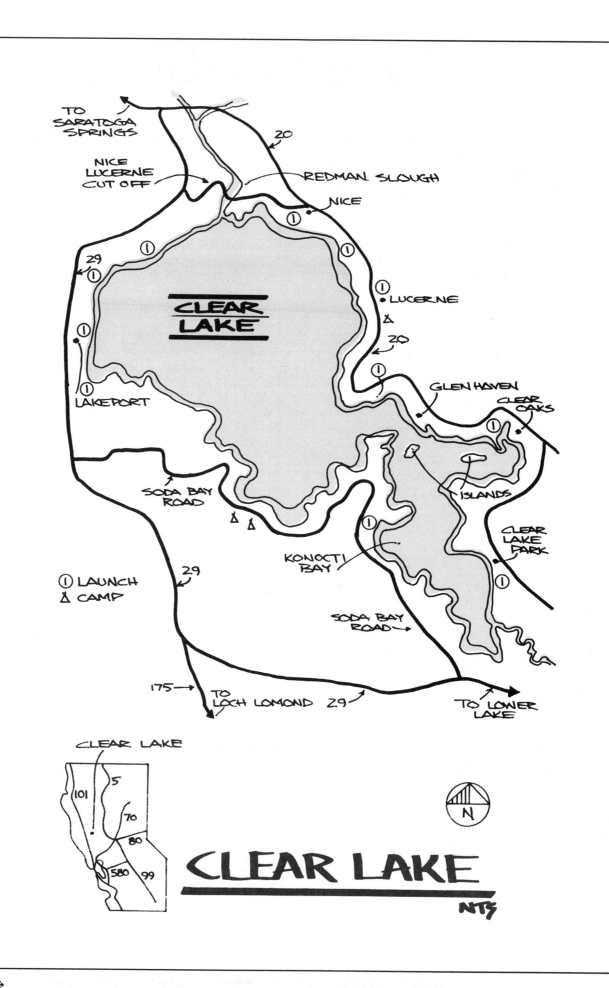

TO SARATOGA SPRINGS

NICE LUCERNE CUT OFF

REDMAN SLOUGH

20

NICE

① LUCERNE

29

① CLEAR LAKE

LAKEPORT

SODA BAY ROAD

① LAUNCH
△ CAMP

29

175 →

TO LOCH LOMOND

29

20

GLEN HAVEN

CLEAR OAKS

ISLANDS

CLEAR LAKE PARK

KONOCTI BAY

SODA BAY ROAD →

TO LOWER LAKE

CLEAR LAKE

101
5
70
80
580
99

N

CLEAR LAKE

NTS

Clear Lake

Clear Lake is actually green in color despite being one of the largest natural fresh water lakes in the state. The gamefish in this water have it all, and on a silver platter: human-built cover, natural cover and an amazingly healthy food chain including large baitfish populations, excellent insect life, even thick algae! Everything is in place for a trophy warm water fishery. If you like this type of lake fly fishing (with plenty of resorts, marinas, camping and boating) don't miss Clear Lake.

Clear Lake is best fly fished from the shoreline, of which there is over 100 miles. Stick to the tule-lined sections that harbor panfish and bass. The lake's many pilings are magnets for trophy black crappie up to 16 inches. Largemouth bass also prowl these environs while chowing down on the schooling bait *and* panfish. When the bite is on (and you have to be there to believe it) Clear Lake is a hog hunter's delight.

Fly fishing and access is available all year, 24 hours a day. Try working the night bite at least once in your career. It's a real challenge and getting into a big fighting fish you can barely see is quite a thrill. Lights on most of the docks aid those on foot. Boaters must be extra careful at night and slow down in congested areas.

In spring the bass spawning activity around Horseshoe Bend can provide red hot fly fishing. In the fall, even when the surface becomes "slimy", toss poppers into the soup and let it rip.

Clear Lake is 110 miles north of the Bay Area, through the wine country on scenic Highway 29. From Interstate 5 go north to Williams and head west on Highway 20.

Types of Fish
Largemouth bass, crappie and bluegill.

When to Fish
Fish for bass all year with prime time being spring and fall. Summer is best for panfish.

Known Bait Types
Silverside smelt, threadfin shad, crawdads, frogs, newts.

Equipment to Use
Rods: 6-9 weight, 7 - 9'.
Reels: Palm or mechanical drag.
Lines: Intermediate sink or heavier, sinking shooting heads. Floating line for poppers.
Leaders: 1x to 4x, 5 - 10'.
Wading: Wet wade or use hip boots along the shore. Best to fish from a boat or float tube.

Flies to Use
Streamers: Blanton's Flash Tail Series #2-8, Milt's Pond Smelt #2- 6, Purple Eelworm #6, Burk's V-Worms #10, Whitlock Softshell Crayfish #8, Poxybou Crayfish #4-8, Black Woolly Bugger #4, Fire Bellied Newt #6.

Topwater: Swimming Frog #6, Andy's Loudmouth Shad #6, Deer Hair Mouse #4, Chartreuse Diver #4.

Accommodations & Services
Numerous resorts, marinas, ramps, stores and gas stations around the lake. It's all right there.

Season & Limits
General season, consult the California Department of Fish and Wildlife regulations booklet.

Rating
Time your outing to avoid a fishing tournament and it's a 9.

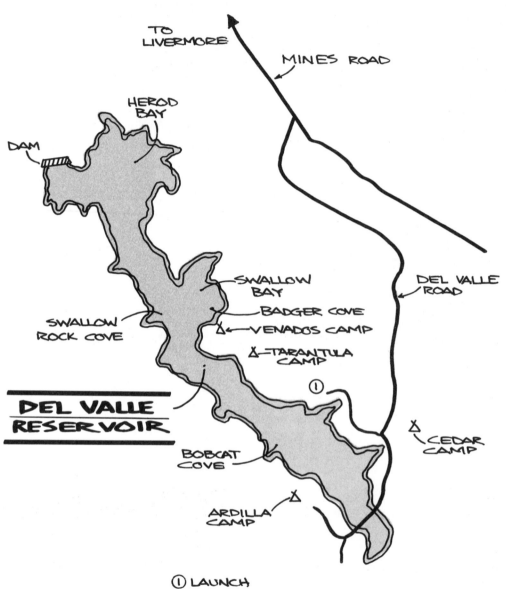

TO LIVERMORE

MINES ROAD

HEROD BAY

DAM

DEL VALLE ROAD

SWALLOW BAY

BADGER COVE

VENADOS CAMP

SWALLOW ROCK COVE

TARANTULA CAMP

DEL VALLE RESERVOIR

CEDAR CAMP

BOBCAT COVE

ARDILLA CAMP

① LAUNCH
△ CAMP

DEL VALLE RESERVOIR

101

5

70

80

580

99

DEL VALLE RESERVOIR

N

NTS

Del Valle Reservoir

Here's a fine body of water, 10 miles southeast of Livermore, within easy reach of the Bay Area. Besides fly fishing, there are hiking trails, boating and some of the few year-round camp sites located near a large metropolitan area.

Del Valle is a long, narrow, canyon-like reservoir with deep water. It's ringed by sheer rock walls, tapering points, small coves and just a few shallow grassy flats. The steep rocky structure provides high quality smallmouth bass habitat. I love fly fishing for the scrappy bronzebacks in the autumn.

There is plenty of trout excitement during the winter. The East Bay Regional Park District and California Department of Fish & Game plants thousands of 10 - 12" trout weekly. The reservoir's cold water keeps them frisky and near the surface, within easy reach for flyrodders. Watch out though, it's not uncommon for a huge striped bass to try to inhale the trout you just hooked. By the way, in 1994 Del Valle Reservoir yielded a rainbow over 17 pounds.

For stripers, take big tackle and fish near the dam. Largemouth stay to the southern territory where there's timber, stumps and warmer water. Their spawning cycle is short. Be on the water in May. The minnow bite in the fall is a real kick when both types of bass are on the attack. The shore side of coves and shallow flats are home to large populations of panfish. Conservation groups and the park district have been adding brush piles and tire rings to improve bass and panfish habitat.

To get to Del Valle head east on Highway 580 to Livermore. Take the North/South Livermore Road south to Mines Road. After about 3 miles turn right on Del Valle Road which takes one to the recreation area entrance.

Types of Fish
Largemouth, smallmouth and striped bass, bluegill and rainbow trout.

When to Fish
Bass: March - Nov., prime time is spring & fall.
Panfish: Summer.
Trout: Winter, prime time is Nov-April. High winds by midday. Flyrodding is best early-AM & early-PM.

Known Baitfish & Hatches
Crawdads, threadfin shad, caddis, Callibaetis Mayfly, Hoppers.

Equipment to Use
Rods: 5-9 weight, 8 1/2 - 10'.
Reels: Mechanical or disc drag.
Lines: Intermediate sink, sink-tip type 3, sinking shooting heads.
Leaders: 1x to 5x, 7 - 10'.
Wading: A boat is the best way to cover this water. Hip boots are OK for bank angling.

Flies to Use
Streamers: Thunder Creek #6, White Marabou Muddler #2, Burk's V-Worm #10, Whitlock Softshell Crayfish #8, Poxybou Crayfish #4-8, Blanton's Flash Tail Series #6-8, Fire Bellied Newt #6, Blue & White Lefty's Deceiver #2-4.

Nymphs: Jansen Callibaetis, Zug Bug #14, PT #16.

Topwater: Dave's Hopper #6, Gaines Micro Poppers #8-10, Sponge Spiders #10-12, Madame X #6-8.

Accommodations & Services
Launch ramp, marina, boat rentals, concessions and campgrounds at the lake. Lodging, gear, groceries and gas are available in Livermore.

Seasons & Limits
Fish all year, but consult the California Department of Fish & Game regulations for any changes.

Rating
A good setting for both beginner and pro, a 7.

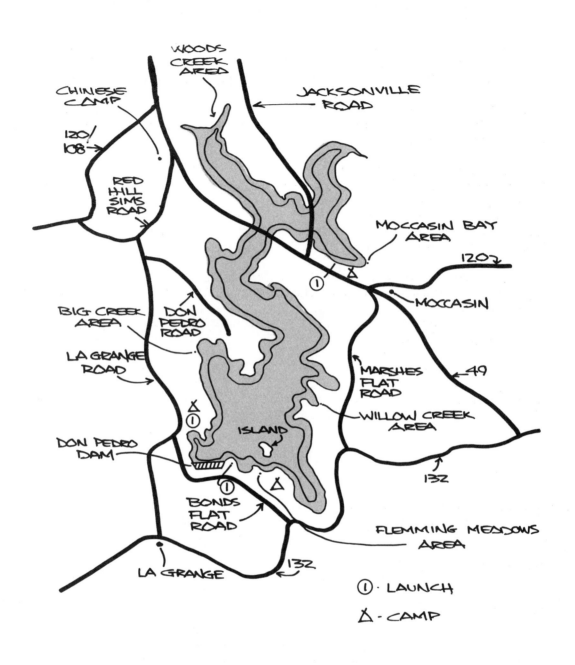

WOODS CREEK AREA

JACKSONVILLE ROAD

CHINESE CAMP

120/
108 →

RED HILL SIMS ROAD

MOCCASIN BAY AREA

120

BIG CREEK AREA

DON PEDRO ROAD

MOCCASIN

LA GRANGE ROAD

MARSHES FLAT ROAD

49

WILLOW CREEK AREA

DON PEDRO DAM

ISLAND

132

BONDS FLAT ROAD

FLEMMING MEADOWS AREA

LA GRANGE

132

Ⓘ · LAUNCH

△ · CAMP

DON PEDRO LAKE

101
5
70
80
580
99

DON PEDRO LAKE

NTS

N

Don Pedro Lake

Don Pedro is one of the best fly fishing destinations of the many lakes and reservoirs in the foothills of Northern California. The Department of Fish & Game keeps the waters well stocked with trout, Chinook and bass, including annual plantings of tens-of-thousands of fingerlings. This is a long lake. The more water you cover, the more productive fly fishing spots you'll discover. Boat traffic decreases the farther you travel up the reservoir's arms.

These arms, coves and inlets are numerous and all have prolific cover. Gamefish have little problem finding and feasting on the healthy food chain in these areas. There are also plenty of places for them to retreat when danger lurks. Way down deep (70'), Chinook salmon patrol the rocky bottom of the main channels. These fish are generally out of reach of even the best fly fishers. There are many trollers on this lake: beware of boating patterns as you explore.

Fly rodders should look for rocky habitat, timber, docks, and points for the best populations of accessible gamefish. The southern coves are teeming with bass. I recommend the Willow Creek and Big Creek areas. Dark colored patterns are classics around these areas. The Woods Creek Arm and the Moccasin Bay area are top choices for trout anglers, with the Fleming Meadows area a good second choice (for trout).

Most get to "DP" on Highway 120. Pass through the towns of Manteca and Oakdale heading toward Sonora. Exit onto La Grange Road and go to Bonds Flat Road to reach the southern part of the reservoir. To access the north shore, just stay on 120 through Chinese Camp and continue to Moccasin Point.

Types of Fish
Rainbow trout, Largemouth, Smallmouth and Spotted bass, Crappie and Bluegill.

When to Fish
Trout: All year, prime time is Fall & Winter.
Largemouth Bass: Feb-Sep, prime times are March, April & Oct.
Panfish: Summer, prime time is early Spring.

Known Hatches & Baitfish
For trout & panfish: ants, caddis, callibaetis and midges. For bass: crawdads, threadfin shad, worms.

Equipment to Use
Rods: 5 - 9 weight, 8 - 10'.
Reels: Standard mechanical or palm drag.
Lines: Intermediate sink, or shooting heads (all types). Floating for topwater and trout.
Leaders: 2x to 6x, 6 - 12'.
Wading: Bank angling is possible. It's a huge lake for float tubing. Boating is best.

Flies to Use
Streamers: Burk's V-worm #10, Black or Olive Wooly Bugger, Poxybou Crayfish, Whitlock Eelworm #4, Olive Matuka, Yellow Clouser Minnow #6, Blanton's Flash Tail Series #6-8.

Nymphs: Poxyback Callibaetis #16, Black Ant #10-14, Bug Eye Damsel #12, Gold Bead Bird's Nest #14, Poxyback Trico, Midge Pupa #20.

Drys & Topwater: Haystack Callibaetis #16, Adams #14-16, Madame X #8-12, Royal Stimulator #12, Whitlock's Red Head Popper, Deerhair Mouse #6.

Seasons & Limits
In general, fish year around, but contact local fly shops or the marina for assistance. Also, refer to the current California fishing regulations booklet.

Accommodations & Services
This is a full-service facility with marinas, launches, boat rentals and supplies. Campgrounds and boat-in camping abound.

Rating
Overall, an 8.

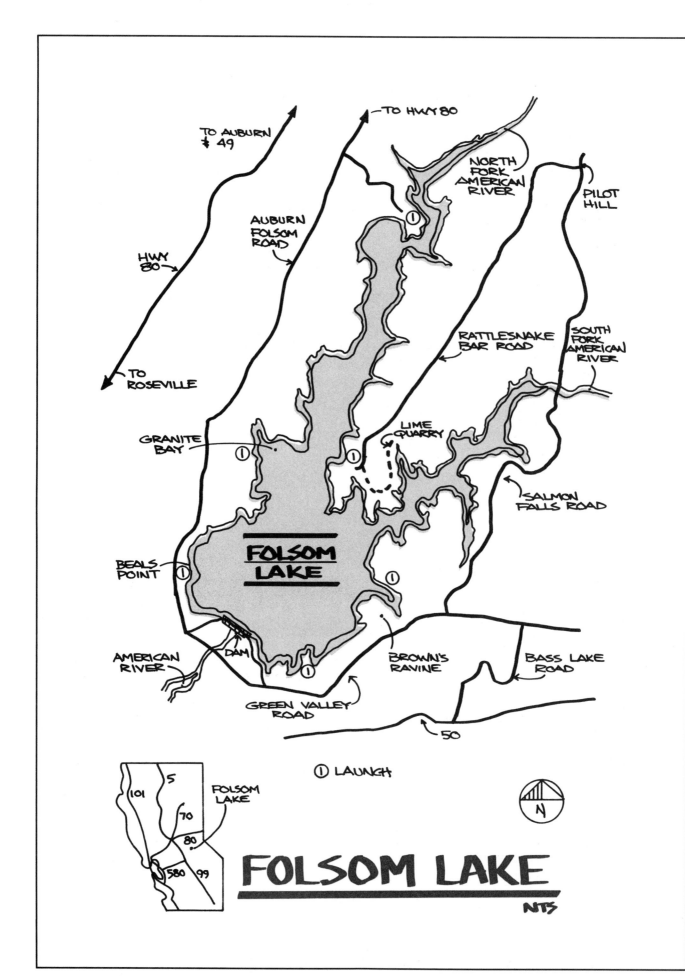

TO AUBURN & 49

TO HWY 80

NORTH FORK AMERICAN RIVER

PILOT HILL

AUBURN FOLSOM ROAD

HWY 80

RATTLESNAKE BAR ROAD

SOUTH FORK AMERICAN RIVER

TO ROSEVILLE

GRANITE BAY

LIME QUARRY

SALMON FALLS ROAD

FOLSOM LAKE

BEALS POINT

AMERICAN RIVER

DAM

BROWN'S RAVINE

BASS LAKE ROAD

GREEN VALLEY ROAD

50

① LAUNCH

5

101

FOLSOM LAKE

70

80

580

99

FOLSOM LAKE

NTS

N

Folsom Lake

Here's a 12,000 acre fishery just minutes from Sacramento where one can fly fish for largemouth and smallmouth bass, and yes, even rainbow trout! The roaring American River provides high quality water throughout the year, though droughts and seasonal conditions affect reservoir water levels. Trout plants begin around November and continue into April. Bass are stocked year-round.

The reservoir has two forks, north and south. The trout love the cooler, oxygen rich water and the North Fork habitat. Smallmouth also like to work this stretch as there's no lack of rocky cover or structure. The South Fork arm also has trout but the emphasis here is the largemouth bass found around submerged vegetation and timber.

The topwater bite, usually an early morning or evening session, is worth pursuing. Chartreuse is a great color selection for this, especially in spring. Fish for crappie near Brown's Ravine. Look for the slabsides to be hanging around brush piles and other structures.

Folsom Lake is about 25 miles northeast of Sacramento. Take I-80 to the Douglas Blvd. exit. Travel 10 miles east to the Granite Bay entrance or take Highway 49 to the marina at Brown's Ravine. Folsom is also a main recreation destination for Sacramento-area fun seekers. On warm days be prepared to share the lake and campgrounds with a lot of people.

Types of Fish
Trout, Largemouth and Smallmouth bass and Crappie.

When to Fish
Trout: Concentrate your efforts January - March.
Bass: March - November, prime time is Apr-May & Oct-Nov.
Crappie: All year.

Known Baitfish
Pond smelt, threadfin, crawdads for bass. Small baitfish for trout.

Equipment to Use
Rods: 6 - 9 weight, 8 - 9 1/2'.
Reels: Palm or mechanical drag.
Lines: Intermediate sink, sinking shooting heads, floating lines for poppers.
Leaders: 1x to 4x, 5 - 10' for bass, 7 - 12' for trout.
Wading: Bank angling in hip boots is possible. Terrific for float tubes and prams.

Flies to Use
Streamers: Blanton's Flash Tail series #2-8, Zonker, Jansen's Threadfin Shad, Purple Eelworm #6, Burk's V-Worms #10, Whitlock Softshell Crayfish #8, Poxybou Crayfish #4-8, Black Woolly Bugger #4, Black Hare Jig #6.

Topwater: Whitlock's Cocktail Hair Popper #6, Deerhair Mouse #4, Chartreuse Diver #4.

Accommodations & Services
There's a marina, 4 public launch ramps, boat rentals, several campgrounds and a store at the lake.

Seasons & Limits
General season, fish for just about all species all year.

Rating
Things can get a bit crazy with summer crowds, but for overall fly fishing opportunities, a 7.5.

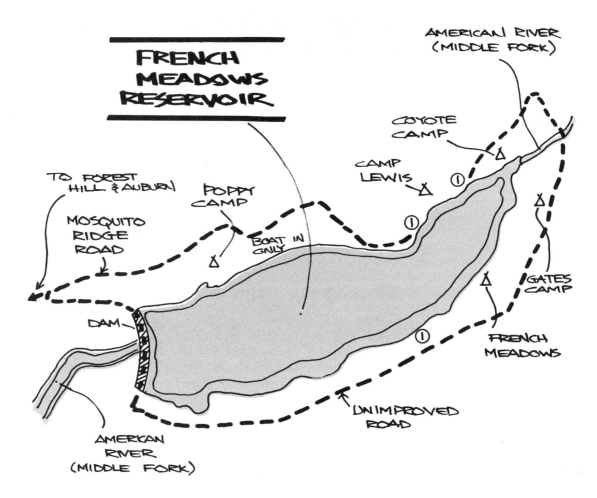

FRENCH MEADOWS RESERVOIR

AMERICAN RIVER (MIDDLE FORK)

COYOTE CAMP

CAMP LEWIS

TO FOREST HILL & AUBURN

POPPY CAMP

MOSQUITO RIDGE ROAD

BOAT IN ONLY

GATES CAMP

DAM

FRENCH MEADOWS

UNIMPROVED ROAD

AMERICAN RIVER (MIDDLE FORK)

① · LAUNCH

FRENCH MEADOWS RESERVOIR

N

FRENCH MEADOWS RESERVOIR

NTS

French Meadows
Reservoir

This Sierra Nevada gem is in a mountain setting and just loaded with trout, trout, trout and trout! They patrol the submerged timber, with stump fields and stick-ups their prime cover. There's a mix of boulders and shelves as well.

The water is usually very clear and planted with over 20,000 rainbows each year. There's also a sizable population of large holdovers. Most of the brown trout are wild and fly fishing for them is real magic in these waters. Adding excitement is the ever present chance to tag a smallmouth bass. There aren't many, but you might find a few around the rocky structure.

The reservoir receives water from the Middle Fork of the American River. Flows are usually restricted in the fall, shrinking the lake considerably. At 5,300 feet in elevation this place can get cold, windy, and down right uncomfortable if you haven't prepared. Don't forget the sun screen either. This is the "real deal" for Sierra foothill trout!

Getting to French Meadows can be tedious, which is one way to control fishing pressure. Get to the foothill town of Auburn and take the Foresthill Road exit. After about 20 miles take Mosquito Ridge Road (turn right). It's about 37 miles to the reservoir.

Type of Fish
Rainbow and brown trout, smallmouth bass, panfish.

When to Fish
Trout: Late May - September.
Bass: June - September, prime time is May-June.
Panfish: Summer.

Known Hatches
Ants, caddis, Callibaetis, midge and minnows.

Equipment to Use
Rods: 5-7 weight, 8 1/2 - 9 1/2'.
Reels: Palm or mechanical drag.
Lines: Intermediate sink, or sinking shooting heads. Floating during calm periods.
Leaders: 3x to 6x, 9 - 12'.
Wading: Use a boat or float tube (canoes are great in the timber). Bank angling is limited.

Flies to Use
Streamers: Black or Olive Woolly Bugger #4, Olive Matuka #6, Blanton's Flash Tail Series #6-8, Yellow Clouser Minnow #6.

Nymphs: Poxyback Callibaetis #16, Black Ant #10-14, Bug Eye Damsel #12, Gold Bead Bird's Nest #14, Poxyback Trico #20, Midge Pupa #20.

Drys: Haystack Callibaetis #16, Adams #14-16, Madame X #8-12, Royal Stimulator #12.

Accommodations & Services
Campgrounds and two launches at the lake. All supplies and lodging in Auburn. Groceries and some supplies in Foresthill.

Seasons & Limits
General state regulations. Consult a fly shop or California fishing rules booklet.

Rating
The access road is long, twisty and lousy, but the fly fishing is great, an 8.5.

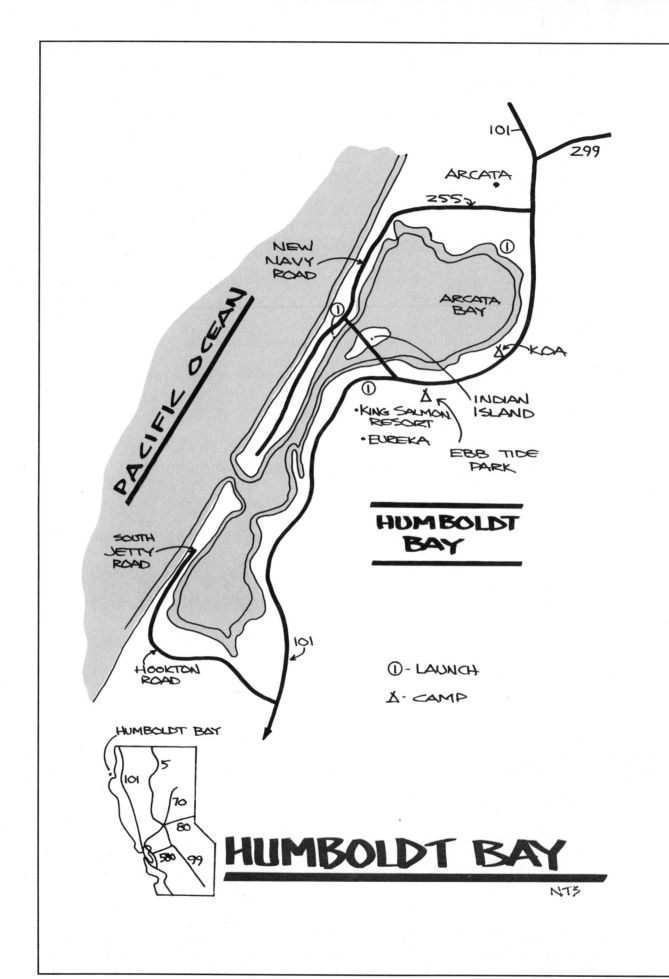

PACIFIC OCEAN

NEW NAVY ROAD

SOUTH JETTY ROAD

HOOKTON ROAD

101

299

ARCATA

255

ARCATA BAY

KOA

INDIAN ISLAND

•KING SALMON RESORT

•EUREKA

EBB TIDE PARK

HUMBOLDT BAY

ⓘ - LAUNCH
△ - CAMP

HUMBOLDT BAY

101

HUMBOLDT BAY

101
5
70
80
580
99

HUMBOLDT BAY

NTS

Humboldt Bay

This is one of California's northernmost (and second largest) enclosed saltwater bay systems. As of this writing, the bay is also a fairly undiscovered salt water fly fishing spot. Two huge spits protect the long inner bay from the pounding Pacific surfline. Shore angler and skiff pilot alike have access to healthy populations of gamefish inside this barrier.

The rugged shoreline protects perfect habitat for many bottom fish. Just inside the southern area of the bay is an artificial reef that attracts Greenling and Rockfish galore. Perch are found throughout the entire system. Fish for flatfish throughout the central and northern areas of the bay. The South Jetty offers challenges for bottom fish and salmon. Night fish along the jetty and you'll probably catch trophy sized rockfish and lingcod. When casting a fly here, use industrial-sized terminal tackle. No whimpy tippets allowed.

If you're looking for a saltwater fly rod outing without much pressure, explore Humboldt Bay. The entire North coast is scenic and worth, what will probably be, a long drive. Take any major highway north to Eureka. The bay and access are west off Fields Landing or Road 255.

Types of Fish
Salmon (Silvers and Kings) rockfish, cabezon, lingcod, greenling, Leopard shark, Starry flounder, Jack smelt and a wide variety of Surfperch, especially Redtails.

When to Fish
Salmon: July - December, prime time is July-Sept.
Bottom fish: All year.
Leopard Shark: All year, prime time is spring & fall.
Starry Flounder: All year, prime time is fall - early spring.
Jack Smelt: All year.
Surf Perch: All year.

Known Baitfish
Smelt, shrimp, crab, softshell clams, marine worms.

Equipment to Use
Rods: 8 - 10 weight. 9 - 10'.
Reels: Large backing capacity, mechanical drag.
Lines: Type 4 sink, or heavy sink shooting heads, 300 - 400 grain. Floating line for poppers.
Leaders: 0x to 2x, 3 - 6'.
Wading: Hip boots or chest-high neoprenes and felt-soled boots for bank angling around Buhne Point, South Spit, Fields Landing and Eureka docks. Limited access at North Spit. A boat is the best way to explore the entire area.

Flies to Use
Streamers: Blanton's Sar-Mul-Mac Anchovy #3/0, Blanton's Flashtail Whistler #3/0, blue, white, all yellow Lefty's Deceiver #3/0-1/0, Popovic's Surf Candy #1/0, Hare Eel, Bendbacks #2, Clouser Minnow #2-6.

Topwater: Pencil Popper #2/0, Salt Water Slider #2/0, Milt's Minnow #1/0.

Accommodations & Services
Camping at North Spit, KOA Campground, King Salmon Resort and Ebb Tide RV Park. Lodging and supplies are available in Arcata and Eureka. Public launch ramps and marina at Fields Landing (south) and north of Eureka.

Seasons & Limits
Restrictions for access, tackle and harvest vary. Refer to current California DF&G Regulations.

Rating
It's wild...and it's worth the trip, a 9.

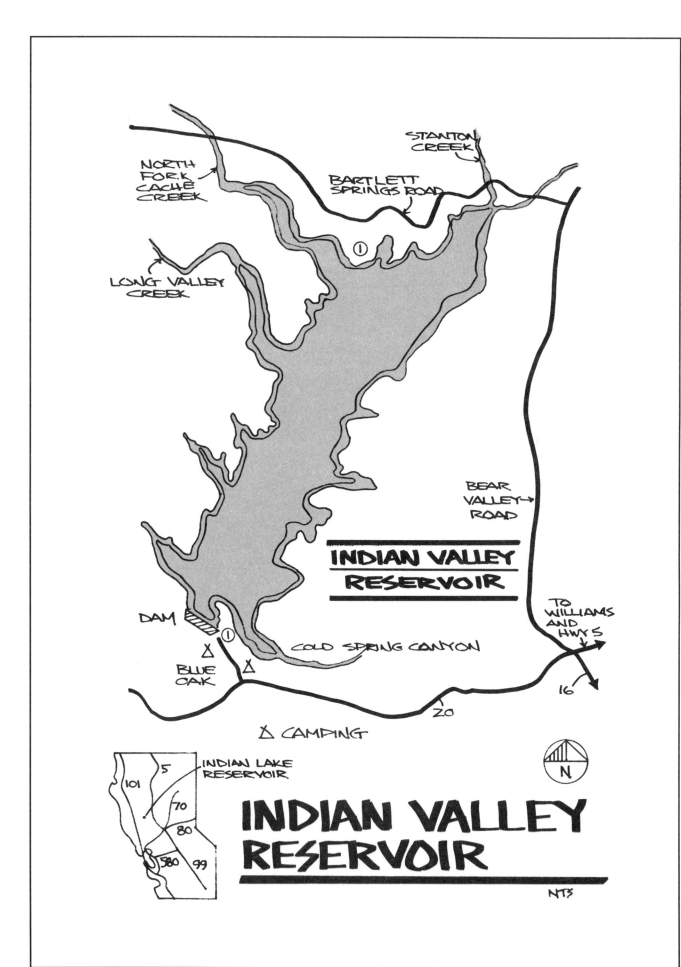

STANTON CREEK

NORTH FORK CACHE CREEK

BARTLETT SPRINGS ROAD

LONG VALLEY CREEK

①

BEAR VALLEY ROAD →

INDIAN VALLEY RESERVOIR

DAM

①

BLUE OAK

COLD SPRING CANYON

TO WILLIAMS AND HWY 5

16

20

△ CAMPING

INDIAN LAKE RESERVOIR

5
101
70
80
580
99

N

INDIAN VALLEY RESERVOIR

NTS

Indian Valley Reservoir

A plain reservoir, but Indian Valley is one of my favorites. The place is all about timber and ambush country for slabsides and bass. There are trout, near the inlets and dam in the cool weather months, but bass is the main object here. The water is usually clear and warm and fun to fish if you don't mind working stumps and stick-ups. You'll need a boat to get around the area, or use it to tow a float tube. Canoes are a tremendous access in the tight cover.

A sink-tip or floating line with a long leader is the best setup for working this vertical fly fishing world. Make presentations in tight, next to the cover. Poppers, making an escape from the timber, can provide dynamite action. With all the wood you'll be casting to, select tippet that's hearty and check it frequently for nicks or damage.

Generally, the best fly fishing is inside the small coves scattered around the lake. Don't forget to work the coves' points. They represent transition zones that bass use all year. You can fish the lake 24 hours a day.

The main problem with Indian Valley Reservoir is access. The last of the roads that get you to the lake are twisty and slow going. A good way to get there is from I-5 and the town of Williams. Take Highway 20 west 10 miles where you'll take a right turn on Leesville-Walnut Road. Just past Leesville take Bear Valley Road left and in a couple of miles take Bartlett Springs Road to the lake.

Types of Fish
Largemouth, Smallmouth and Spotted bass, crappie, bluegill, rainbow trout.

When to Fish
Bass: All year, prime time is spring and fall.
Panfish: Summer.
Trout: Winter.

Known Baitfish
Crawdads, perch, and panfish.

Equipment to Use
Rods: 4 - 9 weight, 8 1/2 - 10'. Consider rod weight when working around the timber. Use lighter rods if you work the open water.
Reels: Palm or mechanical drag.
Lines: Intermediate sink, or sink-tip type 3. Floating for popper work.
Leaders: 0x to 3x, 5 - 9'.
Wading: Best to have a boat or float tube as bank angling is limited.

Flies to Use
Streamers: Olive Matuka #6, Burk's V-Worms #10, Whitlock Softshell Crayfish #8, Poxybou Crayfish #4-8, Blanton's Flash Tail, Bluegill version #6.

Topwater: Swimming Frog #6, dark pattern Whitlock Deerhair Poppers #6, Chartreuse Dahlberg Diver #8.

Accommodations & Services
Two launch ramps, a supply store and rental boats. Some campsites available.

Seasons & Limits
General season. Check a fly shop or the California DF&G regulations.

Rating
I could do without the road in, otherwise, an 8.

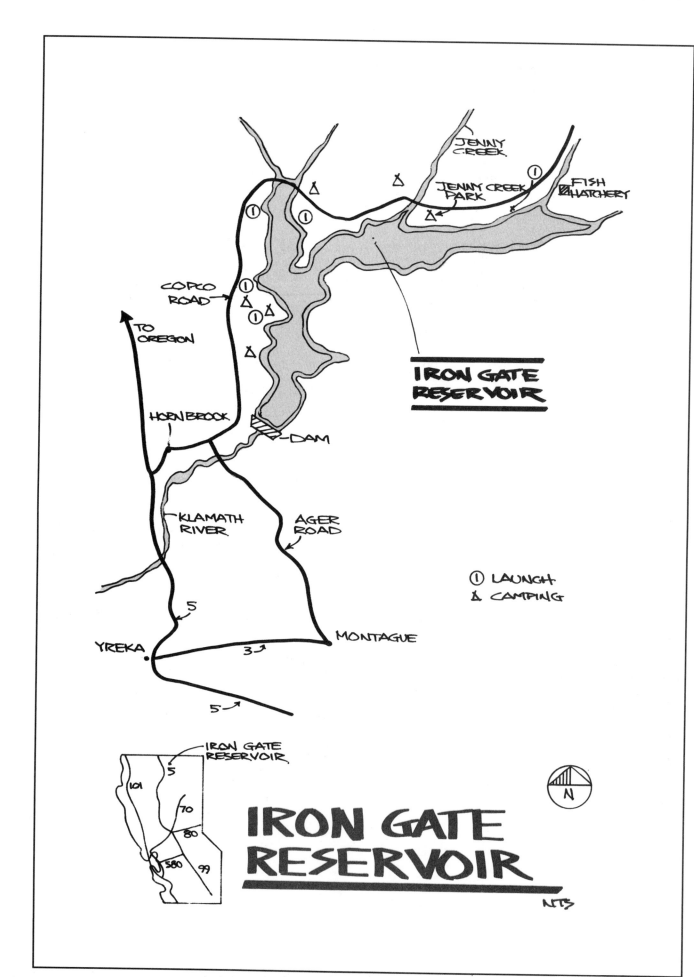

IRON GATE
RESERVOIR

JENNY CREEK

JENNY CREEK PARK

FISH HATCHERY

COPCO ROAD

TO OREGON

HORNBROOK

DAM

KLAMATH RIVER

AGER ROAD

① LAUNCH
⚑ CAMPING

MONTAGUE

5

YREKA

3

5

IRON GATE RESERVOIR

5

101

70

80

580

99

IRON GATE
RESERVOIR

N

NTS

Iron Gate Reservoir

If you want to catch a mess of feisty fish, go to Iron Gate and Copco Lake. There's a bonanza of yellow perch and fly fishing for them is just plain ol' fun! Perch here seem to bite anything sporting a red coat. A San Juan Worm or a sunken Royal Red Humpy is like candy to these fish.

There's plenty of cattails and weeds in the shoreline shallows and gamefish travel and feed there. A boat or raft that can get you just a little ways out on the lake is also helpful. If fly fishing for perch sounds too easy for you, then try your hand at the beautiful steelhead strain of wild trout in the lake. Streamers are the most consistent way to catch these fish. When the powerhouse turbines are releasing water, the food chain gets a boost, and the trout become much more active feeders.

Iron Gate is the lower of the two reservoirs in this area. Copco lake is about two miles, on a gravel road, from Iron Gate. Both waters fish about the same and both have launch ramps and no limits on perch. You get to the reservoirs by almost driving to Oregon on Interstate 5. Just north of Yreka take the Henley-Hornbrook road exit and drive 8 miles east on Copco Road.

Types of Fish
Largemouth, smallmouth and spotted bass, crappie, brown and rainbow trout.

When to Fish
Bass: March - November, prime time is Apr-May & Oct-Nov.
Trout: Late fall and winter and early spring.
Crappie: March - November.

Known Baitfish & Hatches
Bass key on shad, crawdads, pond smelt and sculpin. Trout concentrate on small baitfish also, but big meaty nymphs work as well.

Equipment to Use
Rods: 6 - 8 weight, 8 1/2 - 10'.
Reels: Mechanical or palm drag with lots of backing.
Lines: Intermediate sink or heavy sink shooting heads.
Leaders: 1x to 4x, 6 - 10'.
Wading: Best use a boat or, in the shallows, a float tube. Limited shore angling.

Flies to Use
Streamers: Woolly Bugger #8, V-Worm #10, Black Clouser Minnow #6, Thunder Creek #6.

Nymphs: Fire Red San Juan Worm #8-14, Bug Eye Damsel #12.
Topwater: Gaines Micro poppers #8-10, Madame X #8-12, Royal Red Humpy #12, Elk Hair Caddis #10-14.

Accommodations & Services
Free camping is available around the lake. Try Long Gulch Park, Mirror Cove camp and Jenny Creek Park. Supplies are available at the mini mart at Iron Gate.

Seasons & Limits
There is no limit on perch and one can fish for them all year. Bass and trout seasons and limits change so consult California DF&G regulations or ask at the bait shop.

Rating
For the bass and trout, a 7. For perch, an easy 9.

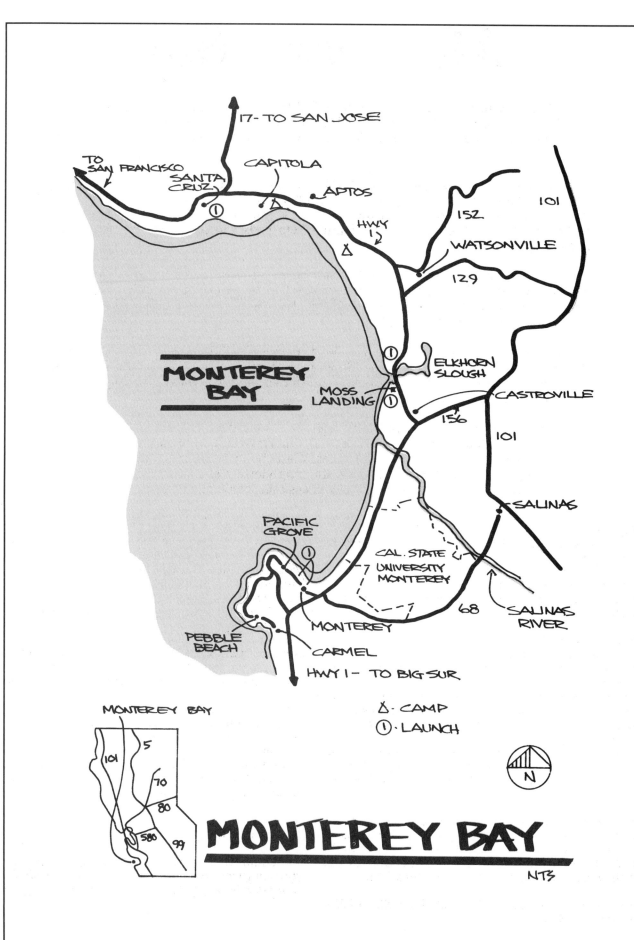

17 - TO SAN JOSE

TO SAN FRANCISCO

CAPITOLA

SANTA CRUZ

APTOS

HWY 1

152

101

WATSONVILLE

129

MONTEREY BAY

ELKHORN SLOUGH

MOSS LANDING

CASTROVILLE

156

101

SALINAS

PACIFIC GROVE

CAL. STATE UNIVERSITY MONTEREY

1

PEBBLE BEACH

MONTEREY

CARMEL

HWY 1 - TO BIG SUR

68

SALINAS RIVER

△ · CAMP

① · LAUNCH

N

MONTEREY BAY

101   5

70

80

580   99

MONTEREY BAY

NT3

Monterey Bay

This bay features some of Northern California's most beautiful coastline. Combine excellent saltwater fly fishing, abundant sea life, famous golf links, resorts, shopping and fun attractions and one can easily find an additional "excuse" to fly fish in this area.

Monterey Bay is a 90 mile crescent from the town of Santa Cruz at the north to Point Pinos and Monterey's Cannery Row at the south. The Bay is home to over two dozen beaches and 40 miles of beachhead. For the fly rodder there are three wharves, two harbors with jetty access, acres of floating kelp beds and plenty of reef structure to explore.

April through November fly fish from shore, as most of the inshore species are available in fairly shallow water. Catch gamefish in the churning surf or in waters from 3 to 30+ feet deep. A small seaworthy skiff is also a good way to fish near shore. Either way one can cast to all kinds of fish.

Striped bass and halibut range from 3-15 pounds. Rockfish weigh from 1-5 pounds. Perch and smelt are typically under 1 lb. though plenty of chunky 2 pounders are available. To tag a shark you'll need a boat to go farther offshore where the pelagic species roam. Blues weigh from 65 to 100 pounds!

Access to the region is from either Highway 1 from the north, Highway 17 over the Santa Cruz mountains, or from Highway 101 when traveling from the south. Take Highway 156, which intersects Highway 1 near Castroville or Highway 68 from Salinas. Coastal Highway 1 from Big Sur offers stunning views, but a slower way to get to the region. Once there, travel around the bay is easy on scenic Highway 1.

Types of Fish
Striped bass, Rockfish, Blue shark, Halibut, Jack Smelt, Surf perch.

Known Hatches & Baitfish
Anchovy, herring, mackerel, smelt, squid, shrimp and crabs.

Equipment to Use
Rods: 8 - 10 weight. 9 - 10'.
Reels: Mechanical and palm drag. Large backing capacity.
Lines: Type #4 sinking line, or heavy sinking shooting heads, 300 - 500 grains. Floating line for poppers.
Leaders: 0x to 2x, 4 - 7'. Lengths will vary with choice of fly.
Wading: Chest high neoprenes with booties for the sandy surf. For hopping around rocks or jetties wear warm, loose fitting clothes and heavy hiking boots.

Flies to Use
Streamers: Blanton's Sar-Mul-Mac Anchovy #3/0, Blanton's Tropical Punch #2/0, Blue/White, Red/White, all Yellow or all White Lefty's Deceiver #3/0 - #1/0, Popovic's Surf Candy #1/0, Bendbacks #2, Yellow Clouser Minnow #1/0-2, Calamari #1/0.

Topwater: Pencil Popper #2/0, Salt Water Slider #2/0, Swimming Baitfish #1/0.

When to Fish
Striped Bass: June-September, prime time is July-Aug.
Rockfish: All year, prime time is Aug-Sept.
Blue Shark: June-December, prime time is August-Oct.
Halibut: June - September, prime time is July-Aug.
Jack Smelt: All year.
Surf Perch: All year, prime time is May - Sept.

Season & Limits
Some restrictions on tackle and harvest exist and vary from time to time. Best to check at local bait and fly shops and in the California DFG regulations booklet.

Accommodations & Services
Supplies and lodging are available in Santa Cruz, Soquel, Capitola, Moss Landing and Monterey. Camping is available at New Brighton State Beach and Sunset State Beach. Public launch and marinas are located throughout the Bay system. Boat rentals in Santa Cruz and Capitola.

Rating
For variety, beauty and accessibility, a 9.

Editors Note: For more excellent information about fly fishing west coast bays and shore lines consult Ken's other fine book, Fly Fishing Afoot In The Surf Zone.

TO HWY 1

• LOCKWOOD

TO KING CITY ♦ WATSONVILLE

18

14

• BRADLEY

NACIMIENTO RIVER

BEE ROCK

19

101

CAMP ROBERTS

BEE ROCK ROAD

OAK SHORES

①

DAM

NARROWS

①

△

NACIMIENTO RESERVOIR

14

SNAKE CREEK

FRANKLIN CREEK

LAS TABLES AREA

PASO ROBLES

TO ATASCADERO

△ - CAMP
① - LAUNCH

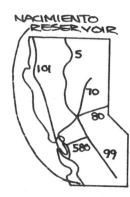

NACIMIENTO RESERVOIR

101

5

70

80

580   99

NACIMIENTO RESERVOIR

N

NTS

Nacimiento Reservoir

Naci can have huge fluctuations of water all year long. Don't let that deter you from this great bass lake though, generally the waters are clear and the fishery unaffected. During the summer there is heavy pressure and traffic from recreational boaters. Twenty-four hours a day angling access, however, makes the summer cycle more productive for flyrodders. The smallmouth topwater bite is incredible to experience during the warmer evenings.

Rocky habitat is premiere bronzeback territory and you'll find it everywhere around this reservoir; mostly along the 160 miles of snaking shoreline. Fish the tapering points around the reservoir's numerous coves and arms. In the Los Tablas Arm you'll find plenty of timber habitat and scads of fish to challenge you. I suggest you take some time to work around the Oak Shores area as well. A successful brush pile restoration program has enhanced this stretch of water.

Most of the bass in Nacimiento are 1 - 4 pounders. The reservoir's lunkers generally stay in the deepest water hugging any cover or structure. Deep water tactics are necessary to catch these prizes.

The White Bass is abundant here. In fact, this is probably the only water left in California with a viable "WB" fishery. During the spring the Whites head toward the Narrows and the river mouth to spawn. When they return to the open lake (throughout the summer) you can find massive schools thrashing the surface during feeding frenzies. Look for surface boils, diving birds, or a ring of boats; any one of these will indicate fish. These little half-pound dynamos can put on a real show for you!

To reach this 5,000 acre compound take Highway 101 toward Paso Robles. Coming from the North, access Naci from the town of Bradley by taking County Road G18, West. From the South take Highway 101, pass through Paso Robles and head to the water on County Road G14.

Types of Fish
Largemouth, Smallmouth and White Bass and Crappie.

Known Hatches
Crawdads, Shad and minnows are the main attraction.

Equipment to Use
Rods: 5 - 7 weight, 9 - 10'.
Reels: Mechanical or palm drag.
Lines: Intermediate sink, fast sinking shooting heads. Floating for poppers.
Leaders: 4x to 2x, 6 - 9'
Wading: Bank access is marginal (private land). Best to work from a boat or float tube.

Flies to Use
Streamers: Thunder Creek #6, Zonker #6, Silver Shad Fly #2-8, White Blanton's Flash Tail #2-8, Janssen's Threadfin Shad #6, Poxybou Crayfish #4-8, Milt's Pond Smelt #6.

Topwater: Gaines Micro Poppers #8-10, Andy's Loudmouth Popper #6.

When to Fish
Smallmouth Bass
All year, prime time is January - March.
Largemouth Bass
All year, prime time is mid-spring and fall.
White Bass
Spring spawn, schooling activity throughout summer.
Crappie
All year, prime time is spring and summer.

Seasons & Limits
General state regulations. Refer to the current California fishing regulations booklet and ask at the marina.

Accommodations & Services
Full service marina, public launch (at both ends of the lake) and boat rentals are available. Hotels in Paso Robles and Bradley.

Rating
For great bass fly fishing in the North/Central part of the state, an 8.

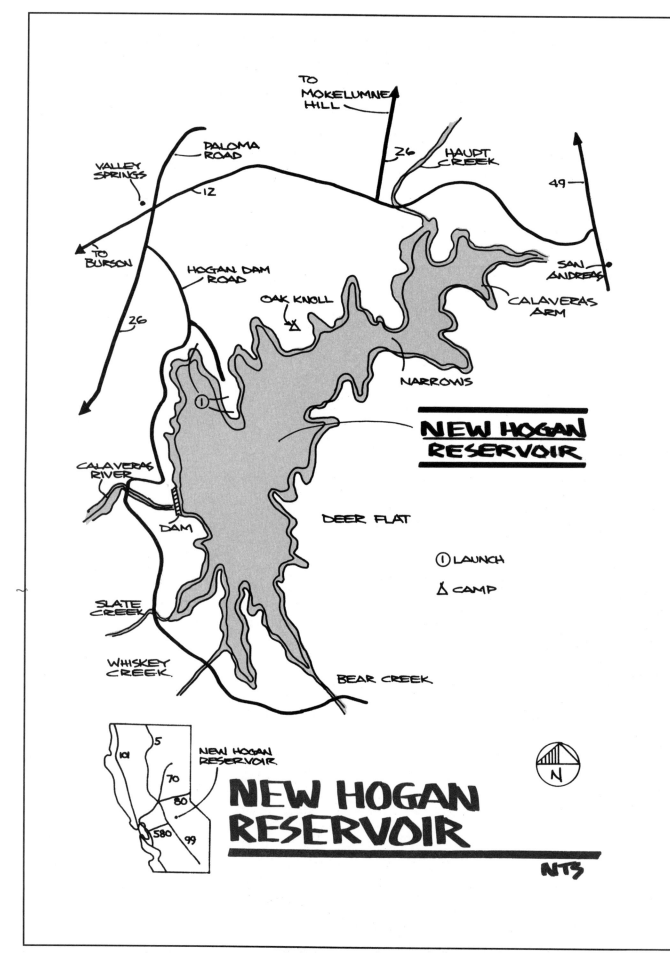

TO MOKELUMNE HILL

PALOMA ROAD

VALLEY SPRINGS

12

26

HAUPT CREEK

49

TO BURSON

HOGAN DAM ROAD

OAK KNOLL

SAN ANDREAS

CALAVERAS ARM

26

NARROWS

NEW HOGAN RESERVOIR

CALAVERAS RIVER

DAM

DEER FLAT

① LAUNCH

△ CAMP

SLATE CREEK

WHISKEY CREEK

BEAR CREEK

101

5

NEW HOGAN RESERVOIR

70

80

580

99

NEW HOGAN RESERVOIR

N

NTS

New Hogan Reservoir

Located in the lower foothill region, New Hogan is just a stone's throw from Lake Camanche. New Hogan is not exactly the hottest ticket for angling, but it can be a good add-on to a foothill fishing and camping tour. In addition, if Camanche is crowded or "off", it's easy to head to New Hogan. The main sport fish here is the striped bass.

Striped bass go on a short topwater spree starting in September and ending late October. Watch for gulls and get your boat in close but not *on* the feeding fish. Trout fishing is most consistent in the Calaveras Arm. Largemouths are usually found in the southern region, around Bear Creek Cove. Boat-in campers will enjoy the quiet coves up the creek arms and in the pretty Deer Flat area. Water-ski congestion can be a problem in the summer and more incentive to explore the lake's quiet arms. The southern arms - Whisky and Bear Creeks - are good choices.

New Hogan Reservoir is in the Sierra foothills, about 40 miles east of Stockton on Highway 26. Travel east on 26 to Valley Springs. From here many local surface roads take you toward the Calaveras River Access. To work the reservoir's northern end, take Highway 12 from Valley Springs toward San Andreas.

Types of Fish
Rainbow and brown trout, striped and largemouth bass and Panfish.

Known Hatches
Caddis, Callibaetis and Midges are available all year. Terrestrials and minnows are tops during the Fall.

Equipment to Use
Rods: 5-9 weight, 9 - 10'.
Reels: Palm or mechanical drag with plenty of backing if you chase the stripers.
Lines: Intermediate sink, or shooting heads (all types).
Leaders: 0x to 4x tippet/leader material, 4 to 10'.
Wading: Bank angling is possible. Boating is the best way to explore the area.

Flies to Use
Streamers: Blanton's Sar-Mul-Mac #1/0, Blue/White Lefty's Deceiver #1/0, Black or Olive Wooly Bugger #4, Olive Matuka #6, Blanton's Flash Tail Series #6-8, Yellow Clouser Minnow #6, Whitlock Eelworm #4.

Nymphs: Poxyback Callibaetis #16, Black Ant #10-14, Bug Eye Damsel #12, Gold Bead Bird's Nest #14, Poxyback Trico, Midge Pupa #20.

Dries: Haystack Callibaetis #16, Adams #14-16, Madame X #8-12, Royal Stimulator #12.

When to Fish
Trout: All year, prime time is in the winter.
Striped Bass: Autumn for shallow-water potential.
Largemouth Bass: February - September, prime time is March - May.
Panfish: Summer.

Seasons & Limits
General state regulations apply, but check at the marina, a fly shop or in the California DF&G regulations booklet for current seasons and limits.

Accommodations & Services
Two boat-in and two drive-in camping areas, public ramp, supplies and groceries, boat rentals and marina at the lake.

Rating
For an easy two-day camping and fishing outing a 5.5.

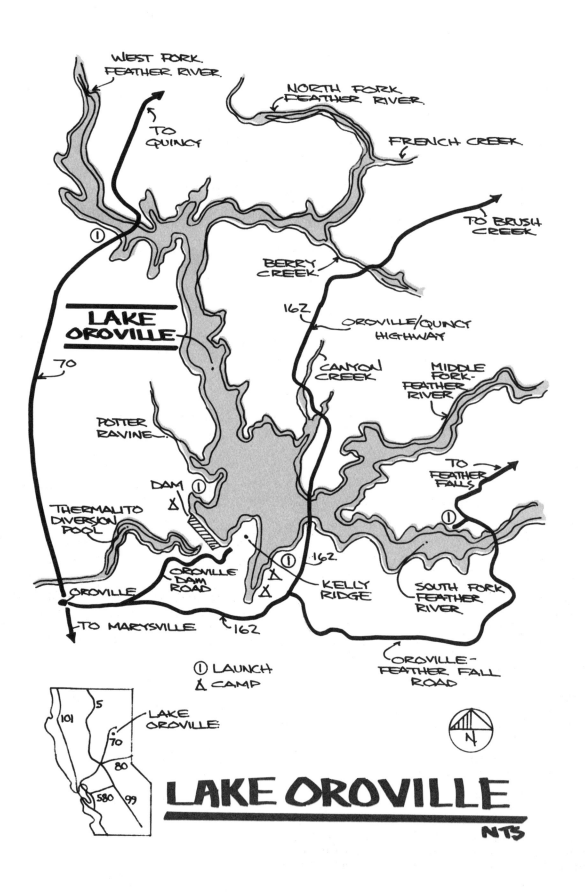

LAKE OROVILLE

NTS

Lake Oroville

Young Lake Oroville has much to offer in the way of fish and recreation. Unfortunately one offering is an inconsistent fishery, at least for the fly rodder. Since 1967, when the dam on the Feather River created the reservoir, huge water releases have hindered fish spawning and propagation. So despite massive fish planting, Oroville's fly fishing greatness is still in the potential stage. Nonetheless, there *are* good reasons to fish here, especially if you're exploring the lake by boat.

Oroville is similar to Lake Shasta; big with steep rocky banks and points that taper down deep. The lakes's three long, narrow arms can provide plenty of private water. When these shallow spawning areas aren't left high and dry (from dam releases) you can experience a fly fishing bonanza. Spotted bass were introduced to partially circumvent the fluctuating water level problem. They spawn in deeper water.

A good way to cast to monster bass is to work this lake at night. Bass, under the cover of darkness, are in the top water and aggressive. Fly fish the structure at Berry Creek, Potter Ravine and the Middle or South Forks of the Feather River.

Trout fly fishing is a bit frustrating here. During warm weather the fish dive deep and out of reach. They're on top when winter turns to spring and when fall turns to winter. At these times, fishing from the shore is possible. Try the West and North Fork arms of the Feather River.

The lake is about 12 miles east of Oroville which is 70 miles north of Sacramento or about 50 miles south of Red Bluff. Take Interstate 5 or Highway 70.

Types of Fish
Largemouth, smallmouth and spotted bass, crappie, brown and rainbow trout.

When to Fish
Bass: March - November, prime time is Apr-May & Oct-Nov.
Trout: Late fall and winter and early spring.
Crappie: March - November.

Known Baitfish & Hatches
Bass key on shad, crawdads, pond smelt and sculpin. Trout concentrate on small baitfish also, but big meaty nymphs work as well.

Equipment to Use
Rods: 6 - 8 weight, 8 1/2 - 10'.
Reels: Mechanical or palm drag with lots of backing.
Lines: Intermediate or heavy sink shooting heads.
Leaders: 1x to 4x, 6 - 10'.
Wading: Best use a boat or, in the shallows, a float tube. Limited shore angling.

Flies to Use
Streamers: Blanton's Flash Tail series #2-8, Milt's Pond Smelt, Zonker, Jansen's Threadfin Shad, Purple Eelworm #6, Poxybou Crayfish #4-8, Olive Matuka #6-10.

Nymphs: Dragon Bugger, Whitlock's Near Nuff Sculpin #6.

Topwater: Whitlock Deerhair Popper #6, Gaines Micro popper #8-10, Royal Wulff #12, Goddard Caddis, Elk Hair Caddis #10.

Accommodations & Services
Supplies and lodging are available in the town of Oroville. There are marinas, public launch ramps and moorings, boat rentals and campgrounds at the north and south ends of the lake.

Seasons & Limits
Fish all year. There are restrictions on harvest and tackle so check at the marinas, fly shops or consult the California DF&G regulations.

Rating
If the drawdowns aren't extreme this can be a solid 7 for the bass fishing, overall a 5.

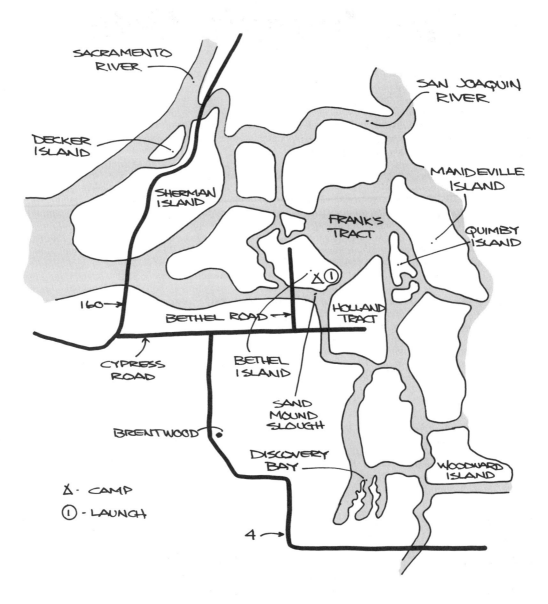

SACRAMENTO RIVER

SAN JOAQUIN RIVER

DECKER ISLAND

SHERMAN ISLAND

MANDEVILLE ISLAND

FRANK'S TRACT

QUIMBY ISLAND

160 →

BETHEL ROAD →

HOLLAND TRACT

CYPRESS ROAD

BETHEL ISLAND

SAND MOUND SLOUGH

BRENTWOOD

DISCOVERY BAY

WOODWARD ISLAND

△ - CAMP

① - LAUNCH

4 →

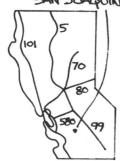

SACRAMENTO SAN JOAQUIN DELTA

5

101

70

80

580

99

N

SACRAMENTO
SAN JOAQUIN DELTA

NTS

Sacramento & San Juaquin Deltas

Deep within the braided waterway systems of the Sacramento and San Juaquin Rivers lies, for the adventurous angler, a fly fishing wonderland. An unbelievable number of cuts, sloughs, islands, and levees presents a smorgasbord of angling locations. The structure and cover varies from tule-lined banks, to grassy flats and channels, and mile after mile of rip-rap styled rocky banks. Much of the fly fishing action takes place in waters 1 to 25 feet deep.

With this much fishing area, variety and proximity to the Valley and Bay Area, the Deltas are rapidly becoming a Mecca for flyrodding: particularly for schoolie and big monster striped bass.

A boat or float tube is really the only way to have success in this area. Angling from shore rarely puts you near the fish. In this region, the more water you cover, the better your chances of finding the "hot" fishing grounds.

Though stripers are the main game fish here, the black bass fishery can be a terrific year-round adventure. The Southwest Delta region, around Franks Tract in particular, is one of the most consistent flyrod fisheries.

Delta Largemouth bass are typically chunky, weighing 2-5 pounds. Do any ten pounders exist? Indeed they do! There's a rich and vibrant food chain that keeps these fish growing.

To reach the Frank's Tract State Recreation Area, take Highway 4 to Antioch and continue past Oakley. Cypress Road to Bethel Island Road will put you right at Bethel Island. Access from the East will be through Stockton, Highway 4 west past Discovery Bay, Brentwood and onto Cypress Road.

Types of Fish
Striped and Largemouth Bass and Panfish.

Known Hatches & Baitfish
This is big bite country. Concentrate on smelt, sculpin, crawdads, grass shrimp, crab and marine worms.

Equipment to Use
Rods: 7-9 weight, 9 - 10'.
Reels: Mechanical and palm drag with 100+ yards of backing.
Lines: #4 sinking line or heavy sinking shooting heads, 300 - 400 grains. Floating line for poppers.
Leaders: 0x to 2x, 4 - 9'.
Wading: Bank angling is very limited. A boat or float tube is a real advantage.

Flies to Use
Streamers: Mullet version of Blanton's Sar-Mul-Mac #3/0, Red/White & Red/Yellow SPS versions of Blanton's Flashtail Whistlers #3/0, Blue/White and all Yellow Lefty's Deceiver #3/0-1/0, Purple Eelworm, Poxybou Crayfish #6.

Topwater: Black Pencil Popper #2/0, Salt Water Slider #2/0, Milt's Minnow #1/0.

When to Fish
Striped Bass: October - December, prime time is October - November.
Largemouth Bass: All year, prime time is Fall and Spring
Panfish: All year

Seasons & Limits
General state regulations apply, but one can fish for something just about any time of year. Contact local fly or sporting goods outlets, or refer to the DFG booklet for species and season restrictions.

Accommodations & Services
Supplies, camping and rental skiffs at Russo's Marina (Bethel Island). Houseboat rentals at Paradise Point Marina (Stockton). Lodging is available in Stockton.

Rating
Overall - 7.5.

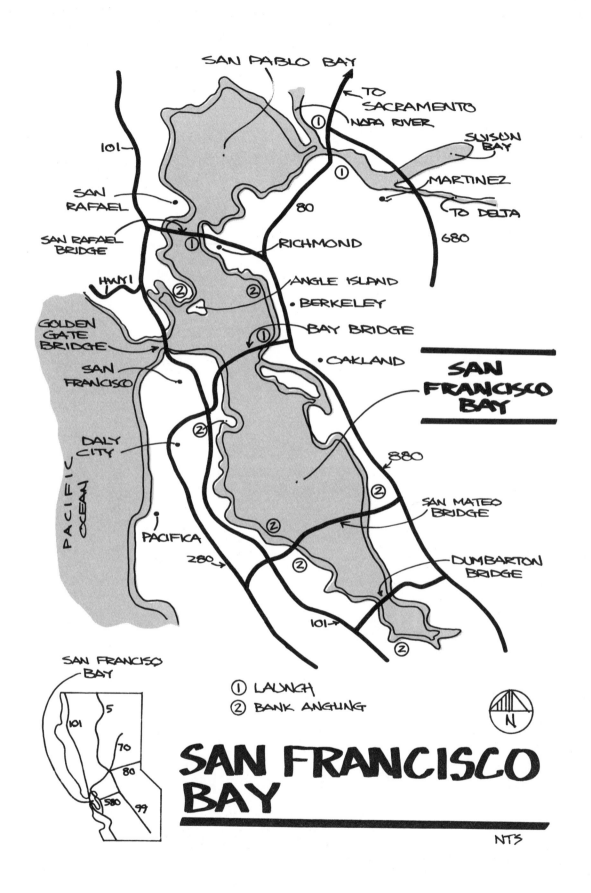

SAN PABLO BAY

TO SACRAMENTO
NAPA RIVER
SUISUN BAY
MARTINEZ
TO DELTA
680

101
SAN RAFAEL
SAN RAFAEL BRIDGE
HWY 1
80
RICHMOND
ANGLE ISLAND
BERKELEY
BAY BRIDGE
OAKLAND

GOLDEN GATE BRIDGE
SAN FRANCISCO

DALY CITY

PACIFIC OCEAN

PACIFICA

280

101

880
SAN MATEO BRIDGE
DUMBARTON BRIDGE

① LAUNCH
② BANK ANGLING

SAN FRANCISCO BAY

N

SAN FRANCISCO BAY
5
101
70
80
580
99

SAN FRANCISCO BAY

NTS

San Francisco Bay

This is the "Inland sea" of Northern California and it's virtually untapped when it comes to flyrodding. It's hard to imagine, that in such proximity to a major metropolitan area, there is a place as alive with wild spirited critters as this bay. You can fly fish for stripers, shark, flatfish or rockfish. Perch and smelt will even take after your streamer! I urge you to pick up your fly rod and join in the early stages of exploration of this great fly fishing opportunity.

One of the keys to successful outings will be coordinating your trip with the tide table. The best potential occurs during moving water, and the greatest exchange of water occurs during a spring tide (new or full moon phases). Choose the days where you'll experience the maximum swing from low to high tide and back again. The tidal shift and resulting currents will stir the baitfish and food chain, creating a more aggressive feeding session for the top-end predators that patrol the bay.

Bank anglers use access from municipal piers, docks and the varied shorelines. Habitat ranges from mud flats and sloughs, rip rap and rock piers, dikes, bridges and other structures. Fly fish in the San Mateo, Burlingame, Berkeley, Sausalito, Milpitas and Hayward areas. Some exploration, however, may yield good new and untested spots no one has heard of.

You can work the Bay 24 hours a day if you're on foot and on one of these projections or shores. Topwater action is good throughout the nighttime bite. Working from a boat is a huge advantage. Note that fishing from boats or any free floating platform at night is not allowed.

San Francisco Bay has an average depth of about 20', with large tracts of mud flats that average less than 10'. Most of the Bay system is well within the limits of fly tackle. There are a few exceptions, most notably the shipping lanes. Obviously these deep waters are not very fly fishing friendly and should be avoided!

Types of Fish
Striped bass, Leopard shark, halibut, smelt and perch.

Known Hatches & Baitfish
Smelt, anchovy, shrimp, crab, softshell clam and marine worm.

Equipment to Use
Rods: 8 - 10 weight, 9 - 10'.
Reels: Mechanical drag. Large backing capacity: these fish are strong and have a lot of room to move.
Lines: Type 4 sinking or heavy sinking shooting heads. Floating line for poppers.
Leaders: 0x to 2x, 3 - 7'. Lengths vary with fly presentation.
Wading: Bank angling, in sturdy shoes, is easiest around San Mateo, Burlingame, Berkeley, Sausalito, Milpitas and Hayward. Best to work from a boat.

Flies to Use
Streamers: Blanton's Sar-Mul-Mac Anchovy #3/0, Blanton's Flashtail Whistler #3/0, Blue/White and all Yellow Lefty's Deceiver #3/0 - 1/0, Popovic's Surf Candy #1/0, Hare Eel #2, Bendbacks #2, Mini Puffs #4, Clouser Minnow #2 - 6.

Topwater: Pencil Popper #2/0, Salt Water Slider #2/0, Milt's Minnow #1/0.

When to Fish
Striped Bass: March - December, prime time is Aug. - Nov.
Leopard Shark: All year, prime time is spring and fall.
Halibut: June - September, prime time is June - August.
Smelt: All year.
Perch: All year.

Seasons & Limits
Restrictions for access, tackle and harvest do change. Things can become complicated. Consult the DF&G regulations booklet for current regulations.

Accommodations & Services
Supplies and lodging are available throughout the San Francisco Bay Area. Public launch and marinas are located throughout the Bay system.

Rating
This is a real treat for intrepid fly fishiners. Convenience and lots of fish, overall a 7.

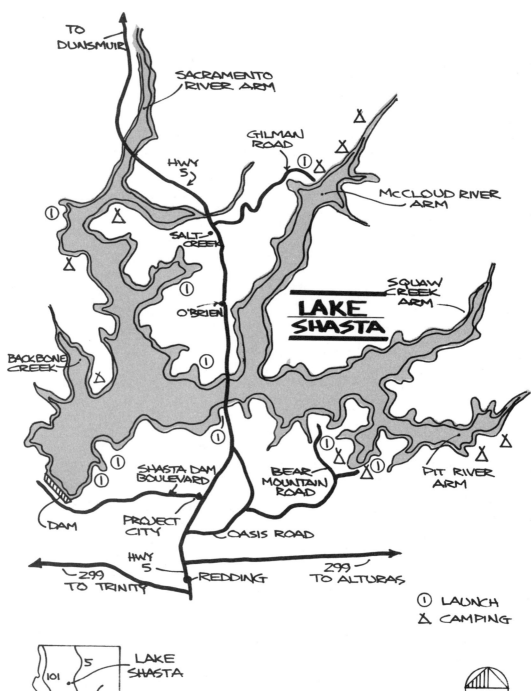

TO DUNSMUIR

SACRAMENTO RIVER ARM

GILMAN ROAD

HWY 5

McCLOUD RIVER ARM

SALT CREEK

O'BRIEN

SQUAW CREEK ARM

LAKE SHASTA

BACKBONE CREEK

PIT RIVER ARM

SHASTA DAM BOULEVARD

BEAR MOUNTAIN ROAD

DAM

PROJECT CITY

OASIS ROAD

HWY 5

299 TO TRINITY

REDDING

299 TO ALTURAS

Ⓘ LAUNCH
△ CAMPING

LAKE SHASTA

101 5
LAKE SHASTA
70
80
580 99

N

LAKE SHASTA

NTS

Lake Shasta

This place is immense! There's over 365 miles of shoreline and over 29,000 acres of surface water covering four huge river canyons. Full service marinas, launch areas, campgrounds, even floating bathroom facilities offer convenience for everyone. And this reservoir kicks out gamefish all year.

Shasta has steep and deep banks, small coves, rocky points, and submerged timber. Work along the face of the dam too. Upwelling provides consistent food supplies for aggressive fish. Use extra caution boating during a fishing tournament and on weekends.

Be prepared to cover lots of water anytime you fish Shasta. The main arms harbor gamefish: the Backbone and Pit, Sacramento, McCloud and Squaw Creek arms are the best areas for fly fishing. The central lake, over 500 feet deep, is too vast for a fly rod.

Early spring and early fall are the best months for a mixed bag of bass and trout. Fish are found at the surface and to a depth of 20 feet. In summer trout hang around the mouths of tributaries. Large schools of crappie are around submerged timber, especially in the Pit River arm.

House boating, water skiing and plain old recreating attract hundreds of visitors to Lake Shasta, especially in summer. Don't let this discourage you because there's room for all. Shasta is a few miles north of Redding and easily reached off Interstate 5.

Types of Fish
Brown and rainbow trout, smallmouth, largemouth and spotted bass and Crappie.

Known Baitfish & Hatches
Threadfin Shad and crawdads are the tops in this fishery. Check spinner falls and various hatches near the tributaries.

Equipment to Use
Rods: 7 - 8 weight, 8 1/2 - 10'.
Reels: Mechanical drag with lots of backing.
Lines: Sink or heavy sink shooting heads. Floating line for poppers, dries and shallow nymphing.
Leaders: 1x to 5x, 6 - 12'.
Wading: Best to work the lake from a boat though bank angling is possible most everywhere.

Flies to Use
Streamers: White Marabou Muddler, Zonker, Purple Eelworm, Bullet Head Streamer #6, Jansen's Threadfin Shad #6-12, V-Worms #10, Poxybou Crayfish #4-8, Black Woolly Bugger #4, Chartreuse Clouser Minnow #6-8.

Nymphs: Poxyback Callibaetis #16, Black Ant #10, Dragon Bugger, Whitlock's Near Nuff Sculpin #6.
Topwater: Andy's Loudmouth Shad, Whitlock Deerhair Popper #6, Gaines Micro Poppers #8-10, Elk Hair Caddis #10.

When to Fish
Bass: March - October, prime time is Apr-May & Sept-Oct.
Trout: Late winter - fall, prime time is Mar-Apr and Oct-Nov.
Crappie: April - October, prime time is summer.

Seasons & Limits
General state regulations with some harvest restrictions. Check at the bait and fly shops and in the California DF&G regulations booklet.

Accommodations & Services
Supplies, lodging, camping, boat rentals, launches, they're all available lakeside!

Rating
Overall, an 8.5.

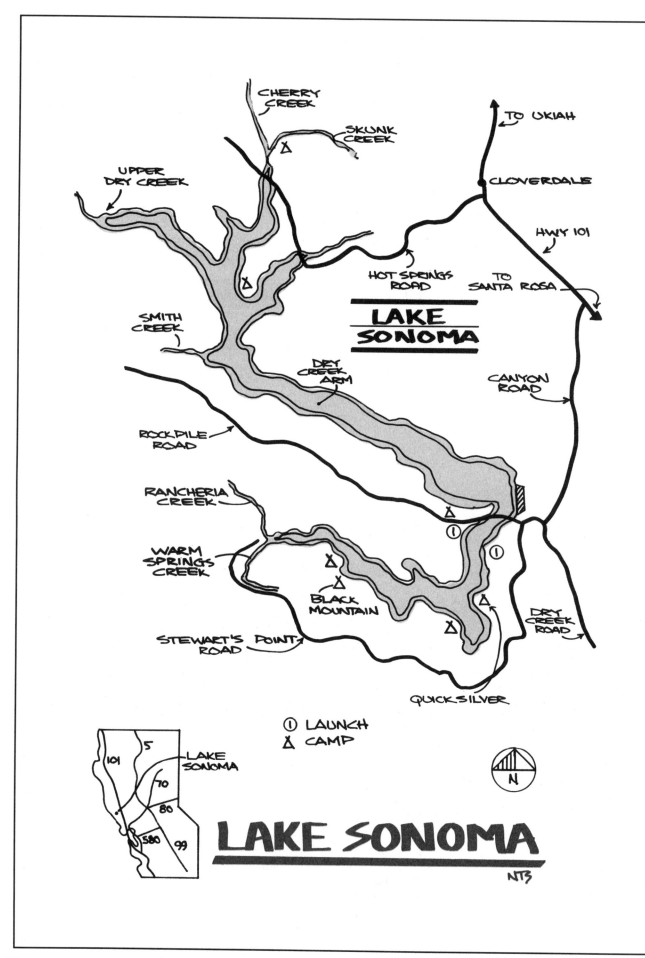

LAKE SONOMA

① LAUNCH
△ CAMP

LAKE SONOMA

NTS

Lake Sonoma

Located in the lovely coastal foothills north of Santa Rosa, this nearby gem is known for sizzling bass fly fishing. There's plenty of structure and cover such as timber "stickups" and submerged vegetation; classic bass habitat where the fish breed and feed. This is all by design.

Lake Sonoma, behind the Warm Springs Dam, finished filling a two creek drainage in 1985. Much of the brush and vegetation was left, creating an excellent warm water environment for fish and fly fishers. Some of the holdover steelhead trout can be caught. They're a minor concern, however, and generally limited to the very deep water at the Dam. Concentrate on the bass and sunfish. Water skiing is restricted to the central body of water further improving the fishing environments.

Most of the shoreline at Lake Sonoma is good bass water. Most of the coves are great bass water. And there are hundreds of coves. Threadfin shad is the main forage for the largemouth bass and the landlocked steelhead. The aggressive smallmouth prefer crawdads and meaty nymphs. If you want to concentrate on the topwater bite, try Skunk Creek Cove and Upper Dry Creek. Other good bass locations include the areas near Quicksilver and Black Mountain camps.

As with most bass fisheries, you'll find much of the action below the surface. Sinking shooting heads can help you probe the deeper water. When boating or tubing, be cautious around all the sunken wood.

Lake Sonoma is off Highway 101 at Canyon Road in the town of Geyservill. Canyon Road turns into Dry Creek Road and takes one right to the lake. From the coast, the lake is a good day trip if vacationing at nearby Sea Ranch or Bodega Bay.

Types of Fish
Smallmouth and largemouth bass, redear sunfish and some landlocked steelhead.

Known Hatches & Baitfish
Bass: Crawdads, minnows leeches, dragonfly nymphs and frogs.
Sunfish Small nymphs, mini-poppers and jigs.
Steelhead Minnow-style streamers.

Equipment to Use
Rods: 4 - 8 weight, 8 1/2 -10'.
Reels: Mechanical or palm drag with lots of backing.
Lines: Full floating, or sinking tip.
Leaders: 0x to 2x, 7 -10' for steelhead.
3x to 4x, 7 - 9' for bass and sunfish.
Wading: Best to work the lake from a boat. Wading not recommended.

Flies to Use
Streamers: Zonker, Jansen's Threadfin Shad, Purple Eelworm, Clouser Minnow, Muddler Minnow #6, V-Worm #10, Poxybou Crayfish #4-8, Woolly Bugger #4.

Nymphs: Poxyback Callibaetis #10-16, Black AP #14, Gold Bead Prince #16, Dragon Bugger #6.

Topwater: Whitlock Hopper #6-8, Swimming Frog, Andy's Loudmouth #6.

Accommodations & Services
Campsites all around the lake; lodging and supplies in Cloverdale, Healdsburg and Geyserville. Launch ramp at Warm Springs Bridge and Yorty Creek Recreation Area. Boat rentals at the Lake Sonoma Marina. Small store just south of the lake.

Seasons & Limits
Fish all year. No bass under 12", bag and possession limits vary. Check at the store or consult the California DF&G fishing regulations.

Rating
Steelhead fishing is tough and deep, a 5. Overall, especially with the warm water species, a solid 8.

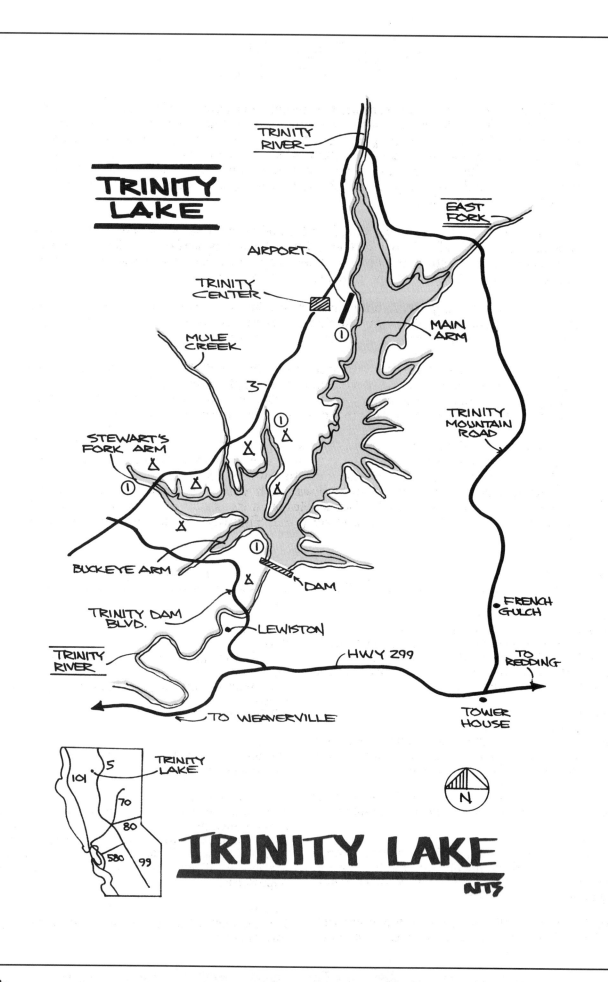

TRINITY LAKE

TRINITY RIVER

EAST FORK

AIRPORT

TRINITY CENTER

MULE CREEK

MAIN ARM

TRINITY MOUNTAIN ROAD

STEWART'S FORK ARM

BUCKEYE ARM

DAM

TRINITY DAM BLVD.

LEWISTON

TRINITY RIVER

HWY 299

FRENCH GULCH

TO REDDING

TO WEAVERVILLE

TOWER HOUSE

TRINITY LAKE

5

101

70

80

580

99

N

TRINITY LAKE

NTS

Trinity Lake

This lake (actually a reservoir) has an amazing number of coves and arms that have sheltered and still water with lots of fish. With over 150 miles of intricate shoreline you'll be busy learning all these fishing waters. Trinity is arguably one of the premier stillwaters of the entire state. Remember, however, that this is at mid-elevation and it can be quite cold here, even on clear average days. An advantage, though, is that many anglers and boaters go to nearby Lake Shasta, leaving Trinity reasonably uncrowded most of the time.

This fishery lays claim to the state record smallmouth bass, a 9 pound 1 ounce brute. In addition, Trinity, also known as Claire Engle Lake, has *tons* of smallies. There's an abundance of rocky structure and cover that they love. The most productive of these regions is the dredge piles in the northern part of the lake.

If you want to tangle with largemouth bass, check in water with vegetative cover. It's more scattered throughout the lake than the rocky structure smallmouth prefer. Submerged willows and stump-studded flats are prime territory here.

Fly fishing for trout can be solid around the streams that enter the lake. Key trout environs include the Buckeye and Mule Creek areas, plus the East Fork Stuart Arm and Trinity River Arm. As the summer progresses, the trout will leave the shallower habitat and cruise the depths making them next to impossible for most flyfishers.

Interstate 5 is the central corridor for access. At Redding take Highway 299 West. If you wish to explore the lake's western shore, travel into Weaverville and then follow Highway 3 to the lake. An alternate route follows 299 west to Lewiston, eventually connecting Rush Creek Road with Highway 3. If you've a little extra time and you appreciate back road travel, take Trinity Mountain Road out of French Gulch. You'll connect with East Side Road and ultimately with Highway 3 at the northern most point of the lake.

Types of Fish
Smallmouth and Largemouth bass, bluegill and trout.

Known Hatches & Baitfish
Smallmouth bass: crawdads and minnows.
Largemouth bass: worms, leeches, shad and "stuff."
Bluegills: small nymphs and mini-poppers.
Trout: Callibaetis mayflies, tan or yellow Caddis, damselfly nymphs, small streamers.

Equipment to Use
Rods: 6 - 8 weight, 9 -10'.
Reels: Mechanical or palm drag with lots of backing.
Lines: Intermediate sink, or sinking shooting heads. Little call for a standard floating line.
Leaders: 2x to 4x, 6 -12'.
Wading: Best to work the lake from a boat or float tube. Bank angling best around the western shoreline.

Flies to Use
Streamers: Zonker, Jansen's Threadfin Shad, Purple Eelworm Bullet Head Streamer #6, Purple or Brown V-worm #10, Poxybou Crayfish #4-8, Black Wooly Bugger #4.

Nymphs: Poxyback Callibaetis #16, Black Ant #14, Gold Bead Prince #10-16, Dragon Bugger, Whitlock's Near Nuff Sculpin #6.

Topwater: Bett's Bull-it Frog #1/0, Andy's Loudmouth Shad #6, Gaines Micro poppers, Elk Hair Caddis #8-10.

When to Fish
Bass
March - Oct., prime time is April-May &Sept.-Oct.
Trout
Late Winter - Autumn, prime time is May and June.
Bluegill
All Summer.

Seasons & Limits
General state regulations. Contact local fly shops or sporting good outlets for assistance.

Accommodations & Services
There are some 400 campsites at the lake. Lodging and supplies in Lewiston and around the lake. For launch ramps and boat rentals try Fairview, Stuart Fork, Cedar Stock, and Estrellita. Cabins are available at Cedar Stock Resort, Airporter Inn Resort, and Trinity Alps Resort.

Rating
For the trout, a 6.5. For the warm water species and overall, an 8.

Got the right fly, Ken?

Photo: Glenn Kishi

Appendix

Northern California Fly Tackle

Far North
Eureka Fly Shop
(707) 444-2000
505 H Street
Eureka, CA 95501

North Coast Angler
(707) 964-6598
260 N. Main Street
Fort Bragg, CA 95437

Reel Fly Shop
(916) 842-6665
614 S. Main Street
Yreka, CA 96097

Trinity Canyon Lodge
(916) 623-6318
PO Box 51
Helena, CA 96048

Trinity Fly Shop
(916) 623-6757
PO Box 176
Lewiston, CA 96052

North Central
The Fly Shop
1(800) 669-3474
4140 Churn Creek Road
Redding, CA 96002

Rising River Fly & Tackle
(916) 335-2291
PO Box 30
Cassel, CA 96016

Ted Fay Fly Shop
(916) 235-2872
4310 Dunsmuir Ave.
Dunsmuir, CA 96025

Trout Country Fly Shop
(916) 235-0705
Dunsmuir, CA 96025

Trout Country Fly Shop
(916) 335-5304
Johnson Park, CA

Clearwater Trout Tours
(415) 381-1173
PO Box 90
Cassel, CA 96016

Shasta Angler
Intermountain Marine
(916) 336-6600
Fall River Mills, CA 96028

Rick's Lodge & Fly Shop
(916) 336-5300
Glenburn Star Route
Fall River Mills, CA 96028

Chico Powell Fly Shop
(916) 345-9983
1154 West 8th Ave.
Chico, CA 95926

Sacramento Area
Kiene's Fly Shop
(916) 486-9958
2654 Marconi Ave.
Sacramento, CA 95821

Fly Fishing Specialties #1
(916) 366-9252
9500 Micron Ave. #129
Sacramento, CA 95827

Fly Fishing Specialties #2
(916) 722-1055
6412-C Tupelo Drive
Citrus Heights, CA 95621

The Tobacco Leaf
(209) 474-8216
123 Lincoln Center
Stockton, CA 95207

San Francisco Area
Fly Fishing Outfitters
(415) 781-3474
463 Bush Street
San Francisco, CA 94108

Orvis San Francisco
(415) 392-1600
300 Grant Ave.
San Francisco, CA 94108

San Francisco
Flyfisher Supply
(415) 668-3597
2526 Clement Street
San Francisco, CA 94121

A-1 Fish
(510) 832-0731
517 8th Street
Oakland, CA 94607

Creative Sports Enterprises
(510) 938-2255
1924-C Oak Park Blvd.
Pleasant Hill, CA 94523

Flies By Night
(510) 538-3861
1015 B Street
Hayward, CA 94541

Fly Fishing Outfitters
(510) 284-3474
3533 Mt. Diablo Blvd.
Lafayette, CA 94549

Pacific Coast Anglers
(510) 830-8791
2005 Crow Canyon Place
San Ramon, CA 94583

The Caddis Fly Shop
(415) 508-0727
1538-D El Camino Real
Belmont, CA 94002

North Bay Area
Fly Fishing Etc.
(707) 762-3073
7 Petaluma Blvd. North
Petaluma, CA 94952

California Fly Shop
1(800) 359-4811
2201 Boynton Ave. Suite B
Fairfield, CA 94533

Western Angler
(707) 542-4432
532 College Ave.
Santa Rosa, CA 95404

Outdoor Pro Shop
(707) 588-8033
6315 Commerce Blvd.
Rohnert Park, CA 94928

Selective Angler
(415) 461-6655
2215 Larkspur Landing Circle
Larkspur, CA 94939

Western Sport Shop
(415) 456-5454
902 Third Street
San Rafael, CA 94939

Sweeney's
(707) 255-5544
1601 Lincoln Ave.
Napa, CA 94558

Novato Sports Headquarters
(415) 897-5388
1300 Grant Ave. at 3rd Ave.
Novato, CA 94945

Wind River Fly Fishing
(707) 252-4900
1043 Atlas Peak Road
Napa, CA 94558

Sportsmen's Headquarters
(707) 996-6299
18700 Sonoma Hwy.
Sonoma, CA 95476

South Bay Area
The Ultimate Fly Shop
(415) 583-1168
494 San Mateo Ave.
San Bruno, CA 94066

The Midge Fly Shop
(415) 941-8871
271 State Street
Los Altos, CA 94022

Mel Cotton's Sporting Goods
(408) 287-5994
1266 W. San Carlos St.
San Jose, CA 95126

Cope & McPhetres
(408)345-2640
2907 El Camino Real
Santa Clara, CA 95051

Upstream Flyfishing
(408) 354-4935
54 N. Santa Cruz Ave.
Los Gatos, CA 95030

Ernie's Casting Pond
(408) 462-4665
4845 Soquel Drive
Soquel, CA 95073

Additional Information

Foothills

Nevada City Anglers
(916) 478-9301
417 Broad St.
Nevada City, CA 95959

Mother Lode Angler
(916) 272-3474
13683 Day Road
Grass Valley, CA 95945

Mother Lode Fly & Tackle
(209) 984-3139
17840 Woods Way
Jamestown, CA 95327

White Pine Outdoors
(209) 795-1054
Arnold, CA

Tahoe

Tahoe Trading Co.
(916) 583-3774
700 N. Lake Blvd.
Tahoe City, CA 96145

The Outdoor &
Fly Fishing Store
(916) 541-8208
3433 Lake Tahoe Blvd.
South Lake Tahoe, CA 96150

Far South

Yosemite Angler
(209) 966-8377
49er Shopping Center
Mariposa, CA 95350

Village Sport Shop
(209) 372-1286
Yosemite Park, CA 1209-372

Buz's Fly & Tackle
(209) 734-1151
400 N. Johnson Ave.
Visalia, CA 93291

Other Fly Fishing Resources

Reno Fly Shop
(702) 825-3474
294 E. Moana Lane #14
Reno, NV 89502

KFBK 1530 AM (Sacramento)
Bob Simm's Outdoor Show
Saturday 5-7 am

KSTE 650 AM (Sacramento)
Bel Lange's Outdoor Reports
M-F 6:25 am

Trout Talk
1(800)AM Hatch
Virtual Flyfishing Radio
Call for stations & times

Ralph & Lisa Cutter's
California School
of Flyfishing
1(800) 58TROUT
PO Box 8212
Truckee, CA 96162

The Fishin' Hole
(916) 791-2248
Bass Specialists
7120 Douglas Blvd.
Granite Bay, CA

Herman & Helen's Marina
(209) 951-4634
Delta Boat Rentals
Venice Island Ferry
Stockton, CA 95207

Walton's Pond
(510) 782-3932
Bass Specialists
23880 Hesperian Blvd.
Hayward, CA 94541

White Fin Charters
(415) 383-2316
S.F. Bay & Delta

Capitola Wharf
(408) 462-2208
Boat Rentals

Santa Cruz Wharf
(408) 423-1739
Boat Rentals

Rivers End Guide Service
(510) 232-9991
Sac., American, Feather Rivers
PO Box 1094
Richmond, CA 94802

North Rivers Guide Service
(916) 469-3492
Klamath & Trinity Rivers
PO Box 404
Orleans, CA 95556

Johnson's Guide Service
(415) 453-9831
Russian, Gualala, Garcia Rivers
69 Bothin Road
Fairfax, CA 94930

Thy Rod & Staff
Guide Service
(916) 587-7333
PO Box 10038
Truckee, CA 96162

Clubs & Associations

United Anglers of California
1(800) 284-3545
1360 Neilsen Street
Berkeley, CA 94702

California Striped Bass
PO Box 9045
Stockton, CA 95208

California Fisheries
Restoration Foundation
(408) 732-8566
160 East Remington Dr. C143
Sunnyvale, CA 94087

California Trout
(415) 392-8887
870 Market Street
Suite #859
San Francisco, CA 94102

The Federation
of Fly Fishers
National Headquarters
1(800) 618-0808
Call for local club

International Game
Fish Association
(305) 467-0161
3000 E. Las Olas Blvd.
Fort Lauderdale, FL 33316

National Fresh Water
Fishing Hall of Fame
(715) 634-4440
P.O. Box 33
Hayward, WI 54843

Government Resources

California Dept. of
Fish & Game
(916) 653-6420
1416 Ninth Street
Sacramento, CA 95814

California Office of Tourism
(916) 322-1397
801 K St. Suite #1600
Sacramento, CA 95814

California Dept. of
Boating & Waterways
(916) 445-2615
1629 S Street
Sacramento, CA 95814

California Dept. of
Parks & Recreation
(916) 445-8513
PO Box 2390
Sacramento, CA 95811

Bureau of Land Management
(916) 978-4754
2800 Cottage Way
Sacramento, CA 95825

United States Forest Service
(415) 705-2874
630 Sansome Street
San Francisco, CA 94111

References & Other Reading

*Ken Hanley's
Fly Fishing Afoot
In The Surf Zone,
For Western Bass, &
Fly Tying & Fishing Guide*
Adventures Beyond

*Northern California
Atlas & Gazetteer*
Delorme Mapping

*Fishing in Northern
California*
Marketscope Books

California Fishing
Foghorn Press

*California Blue Ribbon
Trout Streams*
Amato Publications

Sierra Trout Guide
Ralph Cutter

California Fly Fisher
Magazine

No Nonsense Guides

A No Nonsense guide give one a quick clear understanding of the essential information needed to fly fish a region's most outstanding waters. The authors are highly experienced and qualified local fly fishers. Maps are tidy versions of the authors sketches. The fly shops in the back are excellent places to gather more in-depth fly fishing information.

About The Authors

Harry Teel - Oregon

Mr. Teel wrote the first "No Nonsense" fly fishing guide. It highlights fly fishing in Central and Southeastern Oregon and was published in 1993.

For the better part of 60 years Mr. Teel has fly fished his home state as well as various waters around the world.

After a career with CH2M Hill, Mr. Teel opened and operated The Fly Fisher's Place, a fly shop in the Central Oregon town of Sisters. He's retired again which gave him time to combine his years of fishing notes into a No Nonsense guidebook.

Bill Mason - Idaho

Mr. Mason penned the first fly fishing guidebook to Idaho, published in 1994. It features the best fly fishing waters and showcases Bill's 30 plus years of Idaho fly fishing experience.

Bill helped build a major outfitting operation at the Henry's Fork and helped open the first fly shop in Boise. In Sun Valley he developed the first fly fishing school and guiding program at Snug Fly Fishing, a fly shop he operated for 15 years. Bill eventually purchased the shop, renaming it Bill Mason Sun Valley Outfitters.

Jackson Streit - Colorado

Mr. Streit has fly fished in Colorado for over 23 years. This vast experience was condensed into the third No Nonsense fly fishing guidebook published in 1995.

In 1971, in Breckenridge, Colorado Jackson started the first guide service in the area. In 1985 he opened the region's first fly shop, The Mountain Angler, which he owns and manages.

Mr. Streit has fly fished the western United States, many countries and various tropical islands. He's written numerous fly fishing articles and is involved in various Trout Unlimited activities.

Ken Hanley - Northern California

Mr. Hanley has fished all the waters in this guide. While traveling the world and leading adventure expeditions he's caught over 50 different species of fresh and saltwater gamefish. He's also written much on the subject including three other books.

Ken also writes outdoor related pieces for a variety of magazines and newspapers. This highly enthusiastic speaker also makes presentations to fly fishing clubs and at expos and trade shows.

Taylor Streit - New Mexico

Taylor's guidebook is the first all inclusive guide to the top fl fishing waters in the "Land of Enchantment". Since 1970 Tay lor has been THE New Mexico fly fishing authority and num ber one, professional guide. He's also developed many fly pa terns used throughout the region.

Taylor also owned and operated the Taos Fly Shop for te years and managed a Bone Fishing lodge in the Bahamas. H makes winter fly fishing pilgrimages to Argentina where h escorts fly fishers and explores.

Dave Stanley - Nevada

Fly tier, guide and outfitter, Mr. Stanley is the fly fishing au thority in Nevada. Dave's team won the prestigious 1994 On Fly competition in Jackson Hole, Wyoming. He also guides a over the U.S. and leads fly fishing excursions through out th world.

Dave's business, The Reno Fly Shop, is one of the Sierra most successful. It's the hub of the region's fly fishing informa tion. His guidebook is the condensed version of this know edge. Dave's shop manager and Nevada native, Jeff Cavande (also a top guide) helped organize, write and edit the guide book.

Maps & Artwork

Lynn Perrault - Maps & Covers

Lynn is an accomplished graphic designer who uses tradition tools and computers. She designs No Nonsense guideboo covers in addition to works that have won her many award She was dragged into making maps of fly fishing waters b the publisher.

Pete Chadwell - Flies & Fish

Pete and his firm, Dynamic Arts, provides graphic art service for a variety of clients. As a fly fisherman, he is more tha happy to apply his considerable drawing talents to things tha live and float in and on water.

Notes on Fly Fishing in Northern California

_____

_____

_____

_____

_____

_____

_____

_____

_____

_____

_____

_____

_____

_____

_____

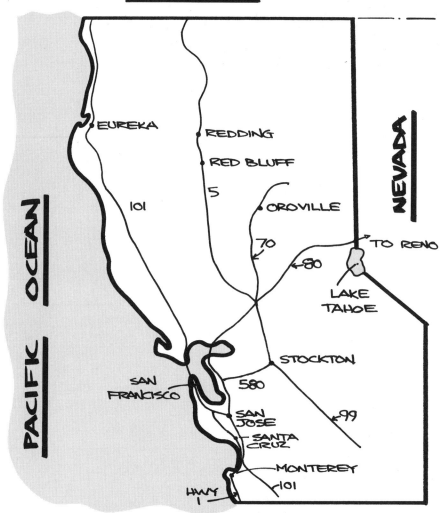

OREGON

NEVADA

PACIFIC OCEAN

EUREKA

REDDING

RED BLUFF

5

101

OROVILLE

70

80

TO RENO

LAKE
TAHOE

STOCKTON

SAN
FRANCISCO

580

SAN
JOSE

99

SANTA
CRUZ

MONTEREY

101

HWY
1

MAJOR HIGHWAY NETWORK

NORTHERN CALIFORNIA

NTS